TO THE GENTILES

To the Gentiles

LESLIE A. FIEDLER

STEIN AND DAY / *Publishers* / New York

First published in 1972
Copyright © 1971 Leslie A. Fiedler
Library of Congress Catalog Card No. 72-81821
All rights reserved
Published simultaneously in Canada by Saunders of Toronto Ltd
Printed in the United States of America
Stein and Day/*Publishers*/7 East 48 Street, New York, N.Y. 10017
ISBN 0-8128-1481-9

Acknowledgments

The author wishes to thank the editors and publishers of the following firms and periodicals under whose imprints parts of this book originally appeared:

AMERICAN JUDAISM for "Marx and Momma," Winter, 1965-66; "Some Jewish Pop Art Heroes," Passover, 1966; "This Year We Are Slaves—Next Year We Shall Be Free," Summer, 1966; "Myths of the Jews on Stage and Screen," December, 1966; "Crimes and Punishments" Spring, 1967.

COMMENTARY for "Prophet Out of Israel," January, 1951.

ENCOUNTER for "Negro and Jew," Summer, 1956.

FOREIGN SERVICE for "Antic Mailer—Portrait of a Middle-Aged Artist," January 2, 1960.

HERZL PRESS for *The Jew in the American Novel,* New York, 1959.

MIDSTREAM for "The Image of Newark and the Indignities of Love: Notes on Philip Roth," Summer, 1959.

NEW LEADER for "On Living with Simone Weil," June 10, 1957.

PARTISAN REVIEW for "Master of Dreams: The Jew in a Gentile World," Summer, 1967.

PERSPECTIVES, U.S.A. for *"Partisan Review:* Phoenix or Dodo?" Spring, 1956.

PRAIRIE SCHOONER for "Saul Bellow," Summer, 1957.

RUNNING MAN for "Some Notes on the Jewish Novel in English or Looking Backward from Exile," July-August, 1969.

Contents

TO THE GENTILES

Introduction

GATHERED TOGETHER here the reader will find all of my essays on Jewish subjects not included in *An End to Innocence* or *No! in Thunder*. I have a strong sense of having said my say on the subject. Doubtless I will be tempted into further comments from time to time on Jewish writers and the world out of which they come, if indeed that world remains distinguishable from the larger community around it. But I think that in no case will I try to preserve such later essays, since in "Master of Dreams" I have come as near as I suspect I ever shall to a final mythical definition of the situation which defines me as well as many of the writers whom I most love. It would be a shame to turn from the central myth to peripheral detail, and I shall try to resist the temptation.

Believing the record of my dealings with the books of fellow Jews necessarily bears witness to the special kinds of difficulties one falls into when speaking *en famille,* I have begun this volume with an essay on Simone Weil (the earliest of the pieces reprinted here) and an account of the troubles that essay caused me. It should be noted further that, though there is no record of it in the text, "Straddling the Wall" was an equal source of *tsooris*. It is, in fact, the only book review I ever wrote in my life which was refused publication, apparently at the behest of the American Jewish Committee whose deepest pieties it offended. Similarly, my essay on the *Partisan Review* brought down on my head actual excommunication, in the form of an indignant letter from the editors of that journal barring me forever from its pages. That "forever" actually lasted, I believe, three years, which seems good enough for a Jewish "forever," and perhaps explains why, despite considerable doubts, I have included an analysis of that periodical and my relationships with it in this particular volume.

The long critical study called "The Jew in the American Novel" has lived a fairly respectable life as a paperback publication issued by the Herzl Foundation; and, in addition, I have cannibalized it from time to time, using pieces of it in certain of my longer works. Nonetheless, I have chosen to include it, since it represents the closest thing I have produced to a continuous exposition of my view of the Jewish American writer. I no longer quite believe everything in it, but I leave it unrevised because I have recorded later changes of heart and shifts of emphasis in the essays which immediately follow it, including those which I did every two months for nearly two years in the pages of *American Judaism*.

The next to the last essay included here moves into the tenderest and most difficult area in which American Jewish literature and American Jewish culture are presently involved; that of relationships between the Jews and Blacks in the United States. The reader will find here a continuation of certain speculations begun in a time which now seems relatively peaceful and innocent, speculations recorded in the essay in *No! in Thunder* called "Negro and Jew: Encounter in America." Taken together these two essays constitute, as I have already warned the reader, a last word on these matters. I see on rereading them, however, that they represent by no means a conclusive one. But to have been anything more or less than inconclusive on this subject would have been not only misleading, but finally not even quite Jewish.

Prophet Out of Israel

SINCE HER DEATH, Simone Weil has come to seem more and more a special exemplar of sanctity for our time—the Outsider as Saint in an age of alienation, our kind of saint. In eight scant years, this young Frenchwoman, whom scarcely anyone had heard of before her sacrificial death in exile at the age of 34, has come to possess the imagination of many in the Western world. Catholic and Protestant, Christian and Jew, agnostic and devout, we have all turned to her with the profound conviction that the meaning of her experience is our meaning, that she is really *ours*. Few of us, to be sure, would find nothing to dissent from in her religious thought; fewer still would be capable of emulating the terrible purity of her life; none could measure himself, without shame, against the absolute ethos toward which she aspired. And yet she does not seem strange to us, as other mystics and witnesses of God have seemed strange; for though on one side her life touches the remote mysteries of the Divine Encounter, on the other it is rooted in a world with which we are familiar.

She speaks of the problems of belief in the vocabulary of the unbeliever, of the doctrines of the Church in the words of the unchurched. The *askesis*, the "dark night of the soul," through which she passed to certitude, is the modern intellectual's familiar pattern of attraction toward and disillusionment with Marxism, the discipline of contemporary politics. The day-to-day struggles of trade unionism, unemployment, the Civil War in Spain, the role of the Soviet Union, anarchism, and pacifism—these are the determinants of her ideas, the unforeseen roads that led her to sanctity. Though she passed finally beyond politics, her thought bears to the end the mark of her early interests, as the teaching of St. Paul is influenced by his Rabbinical schooling, or that of St. Augustine by his training in rhetoric.

Before her death, scarcely any of Simone Weil's religious writings had been published. To those in France who thought of her still, in terms of her early political essays, as a somewhat unorthodox Marxist moving toward anarchism, the posthumous Christian books must have come as a shock. Surely, no "friend of God" in all history had moved more unwillingly toward the mystic encounter. There is in her earlier work no sense of a groping toward the divine, no promise of holiness, no pursuit of a purity beyond this world—only a conventionally left-wing concern with the problems of industrialization, rendered in a tone at once extraordinarily inflexible and wonderfully sensitive.

The particular note of conviction in Simone Weil's testimony arises from the feeling that her role as a mystic was so *unintended,* one for which she had not in any sense prepared. An undertone of incredulity persists beneath her astonishing honesty: quite suddenly God had taken her, radical, agnostic, contemptuous of religious life and practice as she had observed it! She clung always to her sense of being an Outsider among the religious, to a feeling that her improbable approach had given her a special vocation, as an "apostle to the Gentiles," planted at "the intersection of Christianity and everything that is not Christianity." She refused to become, in the typical compensatory excess of the convert, more of the Church than those born into it; she would not even be baptized, and it is her unique position, at once in and out of institutionalized Catholicism, that determines her special role and meaning.

To those who consider themselves on the safe side of belief, she teaches the uncomfortable truth that the unbelief of many atheists is closer to a true love of God and a true sense of his nature, than the kind of easy faith which, never having *experienced* God, hangs a label bearing his name on some childish fantasy or projection of the ego. Like Kierkegaard, she preached the paradox of its being easier for a non-Christian to become a Christian, than for a "Christian" to become one. To those who believe in a single Revelation, and enjoy the warm sensation of being saved in a cozy circle of friends, she expounded the doctrine of a gospel spread in many "languages," of a divine Word shared among rival myths, in each of which certain important truths, implicit elsewhere, are made explicit. For those to whom religion means comfort and peace of mind, she brings the terrible reminder that Christ promised not peace but the sword, and that his own last words were a cry of absolute despair, the *"Eli, Eli, lama sabachthani!"* which is the true glory of Christianity.

But she always considered that her chief mission was to those still "submerged in materialism," that is, to most of us in a chaotic and disenchanted world. To the unbeliever who has rather smugly despised the churchgoer for seeking an easy consolation, she reveals the secret of his own cowardice, suggesting that his agnosticism may itself be only an opiate, a dodge to avoid facing the terror of God's reality and the awful burden of his love.

She refused to cut herself off from anyone by refusing to identify herself completely with anyone or any cause. She rejected the temptation to withdraw into a congenial group, once associated with which she could be disowned by all outside of it. She rather took upon herself the task of sustaining all possible beliefs in their infinite contradictions and on their endless levels of relevance; the smugness of the false elect, the materialism of the shallowly rebellious, self-deceit and hypocrisy, parochialism and atheism—from each she extracted its partial truth and endured the larger portion of error. She chose to submit to a kind of perpetual invisible crucifixion; her final relationship to all those she would not disown became that of the crucified to the cross.

The French editors of Simone Weil's works, Gustave Thibon, a lay theologian who was also her friend, and Father Perrin, the nearest thing to a confessor she ever had, have both spoken of Simone Weil's refusal to be baptized as a mere stage in her development, a nonessential flaw in her thinking, which, had she only lived longer, would probably have been remedied. M. Thibon and Father Perrin are, of course, Catholics, and speak as they must out of their great love for Mlle Weil and their understandable conviction that such holiness could not permanently have stayed outside of the Church; but from Simone Weil's own point of view, her outsideness was the very *essence* of her position. This is made especially clear in the present volume.

"I feel," she wrote once, "that it is necessary to me, prescribed for me, to be alone, an outsider and alienated from every human context whatsoever." And on another occasion, she jotted in her journal the self-reminder, "Preserve your solitude!" What motivated her was no selfish desire to withdraw from the ordinary concourse of men, but precisely the opposite impulse. She knew that one remains alienated from a particular allegiance, not by vainly attempting to deny all beliefs, but precisely by sharing them all. To have become rooted in the context of a particular religion, Simone Weil felt, would on the one hand have exposed her to what she calls "the patriotism of the Church," with a consequent blindness to the faults of her own group and the virtues of others, and would, on the other hand, have separated her from the common condition here below, which finds us all "outsiders, uprooted, in exile." The most terrible of crimes is to collaborate in the uprooting of others in an already alienated world; but the greatest of virtues is to uproot oneself for the sake of one's neighbors and of God. "It is necessary to uproot oneself. Cut down the tree and make a cross and carry it forever after."

Especially at the moment when the majority of mankind is "submerged in materialism," Simone Weil felt she could not detach herself from them by undergoing baptism. To be able to love them as they were, in all their blindness, she would have to know them as they were; and to know them, she would have to go among them disguised in the garments of their own disbelief. Insofar as Christianity had become an exclusive sect, it would have to be remade into a "total Incarnation of faith," have to become truly "catholic," catholic enough to include the myths of the dark-skinned peoples from a world untouched by the churches of the West, as well as the insights of post-Enlightenment liberals, who could see in organized religion only oppression and bitterness and pride.

". . . in our present situation," she wrote, "universality . . . has to be fully explicit." And that explicit universality, she felt, must find a mouthpiece in a new kind of saint, for "today it is not nearly enough merely to be a saint, but we must have the saintliness demanded by the present moment, a new saintliness, itself also without precedent." The new kind of saint must possess a special "genius," capable of blending Christianity and Stoicism, the love of God and "filial piety for the city of the world"; a passive sort of "genius" that would enable him to act as a "neutral medium," like water, "indifferent to all ideas without exception, even atheism and materialism. . . ."

Simone Weil felt that she could be only the forerunner and foreteller of such a saint; for her, humility forbade her thinking of herself as one capable of a "new revelation of the universe and human destiny . . . the unveiling of a large portion of truth and beauty hitherto hidden. . . ." Yet she is precisely the saint she prophesied!

Despite her modesty, she spoke sometimes as if she were aware that there was manifest in the circumstances of her birth (she had been born into an agnostic family of Jewish descent) a special providence, a clue to a special mission. While it was true, she argued in her letters to Catholic friends, that the earlier saints had all loved the Church and had been baptized into it, on the other hand, they had all been born and brought up in the Church, as she had *not*. "I should betray the truth," she protested, "that is to say, the aspect of the truth that I see, if I left the point, where I have been since my birth, at the intersection of Christianity and everything that is not Christianity."

It must not be thought that she was even troubled by the question of formally becoming a Christian; it vexed her devout Catholic friends and for *their* sakes she returned again and again to the problem; but as for herself, she was at peace. Toward the end of her life, the mystic vision came to her almost daily, and she did not have to wonder (in such matters, she liked to say, one does not believe or disbelieve; one *knows* or does not know) if there were salvation outside an organized sect; she was a living witness that the visible Church and the invisible congregation of the saints are never one. "I have never for a second had the feeling that God wanted me in the Church. . . . I never doubted. . . . I believe that now it can be concluded that God does not want me in the Church."

It is because she was capable of remaining on the threshold of organized religion, "without moving, quite still . . . indefinitely . . . " that Simone Weil speaks to all of us with special authority, an Outsider to outsiders, our kind of saint, whom we have needed (whether we have known it or not) "as a plague-stricken town needs doctors."

To what then does she bear witness? To the uses of exile and suffering, to the glory of annihilation and absurdity, to the unforeseen miracle of love. Her life and work form a single document, a document which we can still not read clearly, though clearly enough, perhaps, for our needs. On the one hand, the story of Simone Weil's life is still guarded by reticence; and on the other hand, her thought comes to us in fragmentary form. She completed no large-scale work; she published in her lifetime no intimate testimony to the secret religious life that made of her last few years a series of experiences perhaps unequaled since St. Theresa and St. John of the Cross. If she has left any detailed account of those experiences we have not yet seen it.

Since her death, four volumes of her work have been published in France. *La Pesanteur et la Grâce (Gravity and Grace)*, is a selection from her diaries, chosen and topically rearranged by Gustave Thibon; the effect is that of a modern *Pensées*—no whole vision, but a related, loosely linked body of aphorisms, always illuminating and direct, sometimes extraordinarily acute. We do not know, of course, what M. Thibon has chosen to omit; and he has not even told us how large a proportion of the notebooks he has included in his selection.

L'Enracinement (The Need for Roots) is the longest single piece left by Simone Weil. Begun at the request of the Free French Government in exile, it takes off from a consideration of the religious and social principles upon which a truly Christian French nation might be built and touches upon such subjects as the humanizing of factory work, the need for freedom of purely speculative thought, and the necessity for expunging from our books a false notion of the heroic which makes us all guilty of the rise of Hitler. It is a fascinating though uneven book, in parts ridiculous, in parts profound, but motivated throughout by the pity and love Simone Weil felt in contemplating a society that had made of the apparatus of government an oppressive machine by separating the secular and religious.

The third book, of which the present volume is a translation, is in many ways the most representative and appealing of the three. It is not, of course, a whole, but a chance collection, entrusted to Father Perrin during the time just before Simone Weil's departure for America. It includes some material originally written as early as 1937, though recast in the final years of her life; but in the main it represents the typical concerns of the end of Simone Weil's life, after she had reached a haven of certainty. Among the documents (which survived a confiscation by the Gestapo) are six letters, all but one written to Father Perrin, of which letter IV, the "Spiritual Autobiography," is of special importance. Among the essays, the meditation on the *Pater Noster* possesses great interest, for this was the single prayer by which Simone Weil attained almost daily the Divine Vision of God; and the second section of the study called "Forms of the Implicit Love of God," I find the most moving and beautiful piece of writing Simone Weil ever did.

Another volume of her collected essays and meditations, under the title *La Connaissance Surnaturelle* (Supernatural Knowledge) has recently appeared in France, and several other volumes made up of extracts from her notebooks are to be published soon. Simone Weil apparently left behind her a large body of fragments, drafts, and unrevised sketches, which a world that finds in her most casual words insights and illuminations will not be content to leave in manuscript.

Several of her poems and prose pieces not included in any of these volumes, have been published in various French magazines (notably in *Cahiers de Sud),* and three or four of her political essays have appeared in this country in *Politics.* But the only really consequential study, aside from those in the three books, is her splendid, though absurdly and deliberately partial, interpretation of the *Iliad,* which has been excellently translated into English by Mary McCarthy and published in pamphlet form under the title of *The Iliad: or, the Poem of Force.*

These are the chief sources of her thought; and the introductions to the volumes edited by M. Thibon and Father Perrin provide, along with briefer personal tributes printed at the time of her death, the basic information we have about her life. In a profound sense, her life is her chief work, and without some notion of her biography it is impossible to know her total meaning. On the other hand, her books are extensions of her life; they are not *literature,* not even in the sense that the writings of a theologically oriented author like Kierkegaard are literature. They are confessions and testimonies—sometimes agonized cries or dazzled exclamations—motivated by the desire to say just how it was with her, regardless of all questions of form or beauty of style. They have, however, a charm of directness, an appealing purity of tone that makes it possible to read them (Simone Weil would have hated to acknowledge it!) for the sheer pleasure of watching a subtle mind capture in words the most elusive of paradoxes, or of contemplating an absolute love striving to communicate itself in spite of the clumsiness of language.

Her Life

We do not know, as yet, a great deal about the actual facts of Simone Weil's life. Any attempt at biographical reconstruction runs up against the reticence and reserve of her parents, who are still living, and even more critically, it encounters her own desire to be anonymous—to deny precisely those elements in her experience, which to the biographer are most interesting. She was born in 1909, into a family apparently socially secure (her father was a doctor) and "completely agnostic." Though her ancestors had been Jewish, the faith had quite disappeared in her immediate family, and where it flourished still among remoter relatives, it had become something cold, oppressive, and meaninglessly legalistic to a degree that made Simone Weil all of her life incapable of judging fairly the merits of Judaism. She appeared to have no sense of alienation from the general community connected with her Jewishness (though in appearance she seems to have fitted exactly a popular stereotype of the Jewish face), but grew up with a feeling of belonging quite firmly to a world whose values were simply "French," that is to say, a combination of Greek and secularized Christian elements.

Even as a child, she seems to have troubled her parents, to whom being comfortable was an end of life and who refused to or could not understand her mission. They frustrated again and again, with the greatest of warmth and goodwill, her attempts to immolate herself for the love of God. Her father and mother came to represent, in an almost archetypal struggle with her, the whole solid bourgeois world, to whom a hair shirt is a scandal and suffering only a blight to be eliminated by science and proper familial care. Yet she loved her parents as dearly as they loved her, though she was from childhood quite incapable of overt demonstrations of affection.

At the age of five, she refused to eat sugar as long as the soldiers at the front were not able to get it. The war had brought the sense of human misery into her protected milieu for the first time, and her typical pattern of response was already set: to deny herself what the most unfortunate were unable to enjoy. There is in her reaction, of course, something of the hopeless guilt of one born into a favored position in a society with sharp class distinctions. Throughout her career, there was to be a touch of the absurd in her effort to identify herself utterly with the most exploited groups in society (whose own major desire was to rise up into the class from which she was trying to abdicate), and being continually "rescued" from the suffering she sought by parents and friends. A little later in her childhood, she declared that she would no longer wear socks while the children of workers had to go without them. This particular gesture, she was later to admit in a typically scrupulous bit of self-analysis, might have been prompted as much by an urge to tease her mother as by an unselfish desire to share the lot of the poor.

At fourteen, she passed through the darkest spiritual crisis of her life, feeling herself pushed to the very verge of suicide by an acute sense of her absolute unworthiness and by the onslaught of migraine headaches of an unbearable intensity. The headaches never left her afterward, not even in her moments of extremest joy; her very experiences of Divine Love would come to her strained through that omnipresent pain which attacked her, as she liked to say, "at the intersection of body and soul." She came later to think of that torment, intensified by the physical hardships to which she compulsively exposed herself, as a special gift; but in early adolescence, it was to her only a visible and outward sign of her inner misery at her own total lack of talent.

The root of her troubles seems to have been her relationship with her brother, a mathematical prodigy, beside whose brilliance she felt herself stumbling and stupid. Her later academic successes

and the almost universal respect accorded her real intelligence seem
never to have convinced her that she had any intellectual talent.
The chance phrase of a visitor to her mother, overheard when she
was quite young, had brought the whole problem to a head. Simone
Weil never forgot the words. "One is genius itself," the woman had
said, pointing to the boy; and then, indicating Simone, "the other
beauty!" It is hard to say whether she was more profoundly dis-
turbed by the imputation of a beauty she did not possess or by the
implicit denial of genius.

Certainly, forever afterward, she did her best to destroy what in
her was "beautiful" and superficially charming, to turn herself into
the antimask of the appealing young girl. The face in her photo-
graphs is absolute in its refusal to be charming, an exaggeration, almost a caricature, of the intellectual Jewess. In a sentence or two,
Father Perrin recreates her for us in her typical costume: the over-
size brown beret, the shapeless cape, the large, floppy shoes, and
emerging from this disguise, the clumsy, imperious gestures. We
hear, too, the unmusical voice that completes the ensemble, monot-
onous, almost merciless in its insistence. Only in her writing is Simone Weil betrayed into charm; in her life, she made a principle of
avoiding it. "A beautiful woman," she writes, "looking at her image
in the mirror may very well believe the image is herself. An ugly
woman knows it is not."

But though her very appearance declares her physical humility,
we are likely to be misled about Simone Weil's attitude toward her
own intelligence. Father Perrin tells us that he never saw her yield a
point in an argument with anybody, but on the other hand, he is
aware, as we should be, too, of her immense humbleness in the
realm of ideas. Never was she able to believe that she truly possessed the quality she saw so spectacularly in her own brother, the
kind of "genius" that was honestly to be envied insofar as it promised not merely "exterior success" but also access to the very "kingdom of truth."

She did not commit suicide, but she passed beyond the temptation without abandoning her abysmal sense of her own stupidity.
Instead, she learned painfully the *uses* of stupidity. To look at a
mathematical problem one has inexcusably missed, she writes, is to
learn the true discipline of humility. In the contemplation of our

crimes or our sins, even of our essential proneness to evil, there are temptations to pride, but in the contemplation of the failures of our intelligence, there is only degradation and the sense of shame. To know that one is mediocre is "to be on the true way."

Besides, when one has no flair for geometry (it is interesting that her examples come always from the field of her brother's special competence) the working of a problem becomes not the really irrelevant pursuit of an "answer," but a training in "attention," which is the essence of prayer. And this in turn opens to us the source of a higher kind of genius, which has nothing to do with natural talent and everything to do with Grace. "Only a kind of perversity can force the friends of God to deprive themselves of genius, because it is enough for them to demand it of their Father in the name of Christ, to have a superabundance of genius . . ." Yet even this final consideration never brought her absolute peace. She wrote toward the end of her life that she could never read the parable of the "barren fig tree" without a shudder, seeing in the figure always a possible portrait of herself, naturally impotent, and yet somehow, in the inscrutable plan of God, cursed for that impotence.

However she may have failed her own absolute standards, she always seems to have pleased her teachers. At the *Ecole Normale Supérieure,* where she studied from 1928 to 1931, finally attaining her *agregée de philosophie* at the age of 22, she was a student of the philosopher Alain, who simply would not believe the report of her early death years afterward. "She will come back surely," he kept repeating. "It isn't true!" It was, perhaps, under his instruction that the love of Plato, so important in her thought, was confirmed in her once and for all.

But at that point of her career she had been influenced by Marx as well as the Greek philosophers; and it was as an earnest and committed radical, though one who had never joined a particular political party, that she took up her first teaching job at Le Puy. It was a time for radicals—those utterly bleak years at the pit of a world-wide depression. She seems, in a way not untypical of the left-wing intellectual in a small town, to have horrified the good citizens of Le Puy by joining the workers in their sports, marching with them in their picket lines, taking part with the unemployed in their pick and shovel work, and refusing to eat more than the rations of those on relief, distributing her surplus food to the needy. The bourgeois mind seems to have found it as absurd for this awkward girl to be playing ball with workers as to be half-starving herself because of principles hard to understand. As for crying for a Revolution—!

A superintendent of instruction was called in to threaten Simone Weil with revocation of her teacher's license, at which she declared proudly that she would consider such a revocation "the crown of her career!" There is a note of false bravado in the response, betraying a desire to become a "cause," to attain a spectacular martyrdom. It is a common flaw in the revolutionary activity of the young; but fortunately for Simone Weil, this kind of dénouement, of which she would have been ashamed later, was denied her. She was only a young girl, harmless, and her license was not revoked. Irked at the implied slur, perhaps, and certainly dissatisfied in general with halfway participation in the class struggle of a teacher-sympathizer, she decided to become a worker once and for all by taking a job at the Renault auto plant.

It is hard to know how to judge the venture. Undoubtedly, there is in it something a little ridiculous: the resolve of the Vassar girl of all lands to "share the experience" of the working class; and the inevitable refusal behind that resolve to face up to the fact that the freedom to *choose* a worker's life and the consciousness of that choice, which can never be sloughed off, make the dreamed-of total identification impossible. And yet for the sake of that absurd vision, Simone Weil suffered under conditions exacerbated by her sensibility and physical weakness beyond anything the ordinary worker had to bear; the job "entered into her body," and the ennui and misery of working-class life entered into her soul, making of her a "slave," in a sense she could only understand fully later when her religious illumination had come.

She was always willing to take the step beyond the trivially silly; and the ridiculous pushed far enough, absurdity compounded, becomes something else—the Absurd as a religious category, the madness of the Holy fool beside which the wisdom of this world is revealed as folly. This point Simone Weil came to understand quite clearly. Of the implicit forms of the love of God, she said, ". . . in a sense they are absurd, they are mad," and this she knew to be their special claim. Even unhappiness, she learned, in order to be pure must be a little absurd. The very superiority of Christ over all the martyrs is that he is not anything so solemn as a martyr at all, but a "slave," a criminal among criminals, "only a little more ridiculous. For unhappiness is ridiculous."

An attack of pleurisy finally brought Simone Weil's factory experience to an end (there were always her parents waiting to rescue her), but having rested for a while, just long enough to regain some slight measure of strength, she set off for Spain to support the Loyalists, vowing all the while that she would not ever learn to use the gun they gave her. She talked about Spain with the greatest reluctance in later years, despite the fact, or perhaps because, it was undoubtedly for her, as for many in her generation, a critical experience: the efflorescence and the destruction of the revolutionary dream. From within and without, the Marxist hope was defeated in a kind of model demonstration, a paradigm for believers. Simone Weil was fond of quoting the Homeric phrase about "justice, that fugitive from the camp of the victors," but in those years it was absent from the camp of victor and vanquished alike. Not even defeat could purify the revolution!

While the struggle in Spain sputtered toward its close, Simone Weil endured a personal catastrophe even more anticlimactic; she was wounded—by accident! The fate that preserved her throughout her life for the antiheroic heroism of her actual death brought this episode, too, to a bathetic conclusion. Concerned with the possibilities of combining participation and nonviolence, pondering the eternal, she forgot the "real" world of missteps and boiling oil and ineptly burned herself, a victim of that clumsiness which seems to have been an essential aspect of her denial of the physical self. Badly hurt and poorly cared for, she was rescued from a field hospital by her parents—once more coming between her and her desired agony!

The Spanish adventure was her last purely political gesture; afterward, during the Second World War, she was to work up some utterly impractical plan for being parachuted into France to carry spiritual solace to the fighters in the underground resistance; and she was even to consider at one point going to the Soviet Union, where she could doubtless not have lived in freedom for a month. Among the Communists in France she had been known as a Trotskyite and had once been threatened with physical violence for delivering an anti-Stalinist report at a trade union convention. But at a moment when the Russians were retreating before the German attack, she felt obliged to "add a counterweight" in order to restore that equilibrium which could alone make life here below bearable. One can barely imagine her in the field with the Red Army, this quixotic, suffering "friend of God," flanked by the self-assured killers of "Fascist Beasts," and carrying in her hand the gun that would doubtless have blown off her fingers had she tried to fire it.

These later projects were, as their very "impossibility" attests, different in kind from her early practical ventures: the picketing with the unemployed, the participation in Spain. She had passed into the realm of the politics of the absurd, of metapolitics, having decided that "the revolution is the opiate of the people," and that the social considered in itself is "a trap of traps . . . an *ersatz* divinity . . . irremediably the domain of the devil." The lure of the social she believed to be her special temptation. Against the love of self she was armored by her very temperament. "No one loves himself," she wrote in her journal. "Man wants to be an egoist and cannot." But a nostalgia for collective action seemed ever on the point of overwhelming her defenses. Simply to join together with others in any group whatsoever would have been for her "delicious." "I know that if at this moment I had before me a group of twenty young Germans singing Nazi songs in chorus," she once said, "a part of my soul would instantly become Nazi. . . ." Yet the "we" can lead away from God, she knew, as dangerously as the "I." "It is wrong to be an 'I,' but it is worse to be a 'we,'" she warned herself. "The city gives us the feeling of being at home. Cultivate the feeling of being at home in exile."

Yet charity took her continually back into the world of social action. "Misery must be eliminated in so far as possible from life in society, for misery is useful only in respect to grace, and society is not a society of the elect. There will always be enough misery for the elect." If there is a certain inconsistency in her position, it is easy to forgive. Even the "wrong" politics of her revolutionary youth she would not write off as wholly mistaken; she never repented her early radicalism, understanding it as a providential discipline through which she had been unconsciously learning how to emancipate her imagination from its embroilment with the social. "Meditation on the social mechanism is a purification of the first importance in this regard. To contemplate the social is as good a means of purification as retiring from the world. That is why I was not wrong in staying with politics for so long."

It was after her Spanish experience that Simone Weil reached the critical point of conversion; but the decisive event in her spiritual education had been, she always felt, her work in the factory. She had not known what she was seeking at the machine, but she had found it nonetheless: branded with the red mark of the slave, she had become incapable of resisting "the religion of slaves." In one sense, Simone Weil insisted afterward, she had not needed to be converted; she had always been *implicitly,* in "secret" even from her lower self, a Christian; but she had never knelt, she had never prayed, she had never entered a church, she had never even posed to herself the question of God's existence. "I may say that never in my life have I 'sought for God,' " she said toward the end of her life; but she had been all the time waiting, without daring to define what she awaited.

Taken off by her parents to Portugal to recuperate from her burns and her chagrin, she made her way to Solesmes, where, listening to a Gregorian chant at the moment when her migraine was at its worst, she experienced the joy and bitterness of Christ's passion as a real event, though still so abstractly that she did not attach to it any name. And there, too, she had met a young English Catholic, who introduced her to the work of the British metaphysical poets of the seventeenth century, and so gave her a key to the beyond in the place of conventional prayer to which she had not yet been able to turn.

Like no saint before her, Simone Weil distrusted the conventional apparatus of piety and grace; and it is typical of her role that it was through forms of art acceptable to the most skeptical anti-Christian (Gregorian chant and metaphysical poetry—two of the special rediscoveries of our irreligious time) that she approached her encounter with God. "In a moment of intense physical suffering," she tells us, "when I was forcing myself to feel love, but without desiring to give a name to that love, I felt, without being in any way prepared for it (for I had never read the mystical writers) a presence more personal, more certain, more real than that of a human being, though inaccessible to the senses and the imagination. . . ." She had been repeating to herself a piece by George Herbert, when the presence came. "I used to think I was merely reciting it as a beautiful poem," she writes, "but without my knowing it the recitation had the virtue of a prayer." It is worth quoting the poem as a whole, for its imagery is vital, as we shall see later, to an understanding of Simone Weil's essential thought.

> Love bade me welcome: yet my soul drew back,
>   Guiltie of lust and sinne.
> But quick-ey'd Love, observing me grow slack
>   From my first entrance in,
> Drew nearer to me, sweetly questioning,
>   If I lack'd any thing.
>
> A guest, I answer'd, worthy to be here:
>   Love said, You shall be he.
> I the unkinde, ungratefull? Ah my deare,
>   I cannot look on thee.
> Love took my hand, and smiling did reply,
>   Who made the eyes but I?
>
> Truth Lord, but I have marr'd them: let my shame
>   Go where it doth deserve.
> And know you not, sayes Love, who bore the blame?
>   My deare, then I will serve.
> You must sit down, sayes Love, and taste my meat:
>   So I did sit and eat.

Even after such an experience, this astonishingly stubborn friend of God could not *for more than five years* bring herself to pray conventionally (though she tells us that in 1937 she knelt for the first time, at the shrine in Assisi), finally persuading herself to say the *Pater Noster* daily with so special a concentration that apparently at each repetition, Christ himself "descended and took her." It is her remarkable freedom from, her actual shamefastness before the normal procedures of Christian worship that lends a special authority to Simone Weil's testimony. Nothing comes to her as a convention or a platitude; it is as if she is driven to reinvent everything from the beginning. Of her first mystical experience she writes, "God had mercifully prevented me from reading the mystics, so that it would be clear to me that I had not fabricated an absolutely unexpected encounter." Surely, no mystic has ever been so scrupulously his own skeptical examiner.

Afterward, Simone Weil found in St. John of the Cross and the *Bhagavad-Gita* accounts of encounters similar to her own; and she even decided upon rereading her old master Plato in the light of her new experience that he, too, must have achieved the mystical union. Before her own encounter, she had thought that all such alleged experiences could be only a turning of the natural orientation of the sexual desire toward an imaginary object labeled God—a degrading self-indulgence, "lower than a debauch." To distinguish her own secret life from such *ersatz* mysticism became one of the main objects of her thought.

After her first mystical union, the inner existence of Simone Weil becomes much more important than anything that superficially happens to her. Even the War itself, the grossest fact of our recent history, shrinks in the new perspective. Nonetheless, Simone Weil continued to immerse herself in the misery of daily life. Driven by her constant desire not to separate herself from the misfortune of others, she refused to leave Paris until it was declared an open city, after which she moved with her parents to Marseilles. But there she was caught by the anti-Jewish laws of the Vichy Government which made it impossible for her to teach any longer; and so she went to Gustave Thibon, a lay theologian, in charge of a Catholic agricultural colony in the South of France. Under his guidance, she worked in the vineyards with the peasants (whom she astonished and bored with lectures on the Upanishads!), sleeping as they slept, and eating their meager fare until her feeble health broke down once more. M. Thibon at first immensely mistrusted her motives—a radical intellectual "returning to the soil!"—then became closely attached to her, and it was to him that she entrusted her journals and occasional jottings, which he finally decided to publish after her death despite her request to the contrary.

The chief external influence on Simone Weil during these last years of her spiritual progress was not M. Thibon, but Father Perrin, with whom she was apparently able to talk as she had never been able to before and to whom she communicated what of her secrets could be spoken at all. He was truly and deeply her friend. One has the sense of Simone Weil as a woman to whom "sexual purity" is as instinctive as breath; to whom, indeed, any kind of sentimental life is scarcely necessary. But a few lines in one of her absolutely frank and unguarded letters to Father Perrin reveal a terrible loneliness which only he was able to mitigate, to some degree, and a vulnerability which only he knew how to spare. "I believe that, except for you, all human beings to whom I have ever given, through my friendship, the power to harm easily, have sometimes amused themselves by doing so, frequently or rarely, consciously or unconsciously, but all of them at one time or another. . . ."

It is no evil in them, she hastens to add, that prompts this infliction of pain, but an instinct, almost mechanical, like that which makes the other animals in the chicken yard fall on the wounded hen. The figure of the wounded hen is one to which she returns elsewhere, and in contemplating it, one knows suddenly the immense sensitivity beneath the inflexible surface, her terrible need *not* to be laughed at or pitied for her patent absurdities. One remembers another heart-rending figure she used once to describe herself, "Indeed for other people, in a sense I do not exist. I am the color of dead leaves, like certain unnoticed insects." And the phrases from her journal recur, "never seek friendship . . . never permit oneself to dream of friendship . . . friendship is a miracle!"

It was at Father Perrin's request that Simone Weil "experientially" took communion, and it was with him that she argued out the question of her baptism: Would she lose her intellectual freedom in entering the Church? Did Catholicism have in it too much of those "great beasts" Israel and Rome? Did Christianity deny the beauty of this world? Did excommunication make of the Church an instrument of exclusion? Her friendship for the priest made her problem especially difficult: she did not want to hurt him personally by refusing baptism at his hands, nor did she certainly want to accept merely out of her love for him.

In the end, she decided to wait for an express command from God, "except perhaps at the moment of death." Searching, she believed, leads only to error; obedience is the sole way to truth. "If," she wrote in one of her most splendid paradoxes, "it were conceivable that one might be damned by obeying God and saved by disobeying him, I would nonetheless obey him." The role of the future spouse is to wait; and it is to this "waiting for God" that the title of the present collection refers. Simone Weil finally remained on the threshold of the Church, crouching there for the love of all of us who are not inside, all the heretics, the secular dreamers, the prophesiers in strange tongues; "without budging," she wrote, "immobile, εν υπομενη . . . only now my heart has been transported, forever I hope, into the Holy Sacrament revealed on the altar."

In May, 1942, she finally agreed to accompany her parents, who had been urging her for a long time, and set sail for America. Before her departure she remarked ruefully to a friend, "Don't you think the sea might serve me as a baptismal font?" But America proved intolerable to her; simply to *be* in so secure a land was, no matter how one tried to live, to enjoy what most men could not attain. She finally returned to England, where she tried desperately to work out some scheme for re-entering France and where she refused to eat any more than the rations allowed her countrymen in the occupied territory. Exhausted and weakened by her long fast, she permitted herself to be borne off into the country by well-meaning protectors, but on August 24th in 1943, she succeeded at last in dying, completing the process of "de-creation" at which she had aimed all her life.

Her Method

Simone Weil's writing as a whole is marked by three characteristic devices: extreme statement or paradox; the equilibrium of contradictions; and exposition by myth. As the life of Simone Weil reflects a desire to insist on the absolute even at the risk of being absurd, so her writing tends always toward the extreme statement, the formulation that shocks by its willingness to push to its ultimate conclusion the kind of statement we ordinarily accept with the tacit understanding that no one will take it *too* seriously. The outrageous (from the natural point of view) ethics of Christianity, the paradoxes on which it is based, are a scandal to common sense; but we have protected ourselves against them by turning them imperceptibly into platitudes. It is Simone Weil's method to revivify them, by re-creating them in all their pristine offensiveness.

"He who gives bread to the famished sufferer for the love of God will not be thanked by Christ. He has already had his reward in his thought itself. Christ thanks those who do not know to whom they are giving food." Or "Ineluctable necessity, misery, distress, the crushing weight of poverty and of work that drains the spirit, cruelty, torture, violent death, constraint, terror, sickness—all these are God's love!" Or "Evil is the beautiful obedience of matter to the will of God."

Sometimes the primary function of her paradoxes is to remind us that we live in a world where the eternal values are reversed; it is as if Simone Weil were bent on proving to us, by our own uncontrollable drawing back from what we most eagerly should accept, that we do not truly believe those things to which we declare allegiance. ". . . every time I think of the crucifixion of Christ I commit the sin of envy." "Suffering: superiority of man over God. We needed the Incarnation to keep that superiority from becoming a scandal!"

Or sometimes it is our sentimentality that is being attacked, that *ersatz* of true charity which is in fact its worst enemy, "[Christ] did not however prescribe the abolition of penal justice. He allowed stoning to continue. Wherever it is done with justice, it is therefore he who throws the first stone." "Bread and stone are love. We must eat the bread and lay ourselves open to the stone, so that it may sink as deeply as possible into our flesh."

Or the paradox may have as its point merely the proving of the *impossibility* of God's justice, the inconsequentiality of virtue and grace. "A Gregorian chant bears testimony as effectively as the death of a martyr." ". . . a Latin prose or a geometry problem, even though they are done wrong, may be of great service one day, provided we devote the right kind of effort to them. Should the occasion arise, they can one day make us better able to give someone in affliction exactly the help required to save him, at the supreme moment of his need."

Corresponding to Simone Weil's basic conviction that no widely held belief is utterly devoid of truth is a dialectical method in which she balances against each other contrary propositions, not in order to arrive at a synthesis in terms of a "golden mean," but rather to achieve an equilibrium of truths. "One must accept all opinions," she has written, "but then arrange them in a vertical order, placing them at appropriate levels." Best of all exercises for the finding of truth is the confrontation of statements that seem absolutely to contradict each other. "Method of investigation—" Simone Weil once jotted down in a note to herself, "as soon as one has arrived at any position, try to find in what sense the contrary is true."

When she is most faithful to this method, her thought is most satisfactory; only where some overwhelming prejudice prevents her from honoring contradictions is she narrow and unilluminating—as, for instance, toward Israel, Rome, Aristotle, or Corneille. These unwitting biases must be distinguished from her deliberate strategic emphases, her desire to "throw the counterweight" on the side of a proposition against which popular judgment is almost solidly arrayed; as she does most spectacularly by insisting, in the teeth of our worship of happiness and success, that "unhappiness" is the essential road to God, and the supreme evidence of God's love.

One can see her method of equilibrium most purely in her remarks on immortality of the soul, in her consideration of the rival Protestant and Catholic theories of the Eucharist, and especially in her approach to the existence of God. "A case of contradictories, both of them true. There is a God. There is no God. Where is the problem? I am quite sure that there is a God in the sense that I am sure my love is no illusion. I am quite sure there is no God, in the sense that I am sure there is nothing which resembles what I can conceive when I say that word. . . ."

There are three main factors that converge in Simone Weil's interest in the myth (this is yet another aspect of her thought with which the contemporary reader of Jung and Joyce and Eliot and Mann feels particularly at home): first, there is the example of her master, Plato, who at all the great crises of his thought falls back on the mythic in search of a subtle and total explication; second, there is her own belief in multiple revelation, her conviction that the archetypal poetries of people everywhere restate the same truths in different metaphoric languages; and third, there is her sense of myth as the special gospel of the poor, a treasury of insights into the Beauty of the World, which Providence has bestowed on poverty alone, but which, in our uprooted world, the alienated oppressed can no longer decipher for themselves.

To redeem the truths of the myths, they must be "translated." Sometimes this is a relatively simple process of substituting for unfamiliar names, ones that belong to our own system of belief: Zeus is God the Father, Bacchus God the Son; Dionysus and Osiris "are (in a certain manner) Christ himself." In the fragment of Sophocles, Electra is the human soul, and Orestes is Christ; but in this latter example we are led, once we have identified the protagonists, to a complex religious truth: as Electra loves the absence of Orestes more than the presence of any other, so must we love God, who is by definition "absent" from the material world, more than the "real," present objects that surround us.

In a similar manner, other folk stories and traditional poems can lead toward revelations of fundamental truths: the "two winged companions" of an Upanishad, who sit on a single branch, one eating the fruit of the tree, the other looking at it, represent the two portions of the soul: the one that would contemplate the good, the other (like Eve in the Garden) that would consume it. Or the little tailor in Grimm's fairy tale who beats a giant in a throwing contest by hurling into the air a bird rather than a stone teaches us something about the nature of Grace. And finally, we discover from "all the great images of folklore and mythology" what Simone Weil considers to be the truth most necessary to our salvation, namely, "it is God who seeks man."

The fate of the world, she knew, is decided out of time; and it is in myth that mankind has recorded its sense of its true history, the eternal "immobile drama" of necessity and evil, salvation and grace.

Her Essential Thought

It is no accident that Simone Weil has left behind no single summation of her thought; for she is not in any sense a systematic thinker. Some of her profoundest insights were flashed off as detached aphorisms; and, as we have seen, she sought, rather than avoided, inconsistency. To reduce her ideas to a unified body of dogma would be, therefore, misleading and unfair; yet there are certain central concepts to which she always returned, key images that she might extend or vary, but which she could never entirely escape. These figures which adumbrate the core of her commitment are those of eating, looking, and walking toward; of gravity *(pesanteur)* and light; of slavery, nudity, poverty, and de-creation.

The first group seems almost instinctive, rooted below the level of thought in Simone Weil's temperament itself, and provides a way into the others. The whole pattern of her life is dominated by the concepts of eating and not eating; from her childhood refusal of sugar, through her insistence at Le Puy on eating only as much as the relief allowance of the unemployed, to her death from semistarvation in England, her virtue seems naturally to have found its expression in attitudes toward food. The very myths that most attracted her: the Minotaur, Eve and the apple, the two birds of the Upanishad are based on metaphors of eating; and the final line of the poem of George Herbert, which was the occasion of her first mystical experience, reads, we remember, "So I did sit and eat."

There are two kinds of "eating" for Simone Weil, the "eating" of beauty and the beloved here below, which is a grievous error, "what one eats is destroyed, it is no longer real," and the miraculous "eating" in Heaven, where one consumes and is consumed by his God. "The great trouble in human life is that looking and eating are two different operations. Only beyond the sky, in the country inhabited by God, are they one and the same single operation. . . . It may be that vice, depravity, and crime are nearly always, or even perhaps always, in their essence, attempts to eat beauty, to eat what we should only look at."

Here below we must be content to be eternally hungry; indeed, we must *welcome* hunger, for it is the sole proof we have of the reality of God, who is the only sustenance that can satisfy us, but one which is "absent" in the created world. "The danger is not lest the soul should doubt whether there is any bread [God], but lest, by a lie, it should persuade itself that it is not hungry. It can only persuade itself of this by lying, for the reality of its hunger is not a belief, it is a certainty."

Not to deny one's hunger and still not to eat what is forbidden, there is the miracle of salvation! It is true even on the level of human friendship, "a miracle by which a person consents to view from a certain distance, and without coming any nearer, the very being who is necessary to him as food." And how much more true on the level of the divine! "If [Eve] had been hungry at the moment when she looked at the fruit, if in spite of that she had remained looking at it indefinitely without taking one step toward it, she would have performed a miracle analogous to that of perfect friendship."

It is "looking" which saves and not "eating." "It should also be publicly and officially recognized that religion is nothing else but a looking." Looking, the mere turning of the head toward God, is equated by Simone Weil with desire and that passive effort of "waiting for God" which gives the present book its name; while eating is equated with the will, and the false muscular effort to seize that which can only be freely given. Man's "free will" consists in nothing but the ability to turn, or to refuse to turn, his eyes toward what God holds up before him. "One of the principal truths of Christianity, a truth that goes almost unrecognized today, is that looking is what saves us. The bronze serpent was lifted up so that those who lay maimed in the depths of degradation should be saved by looking upon it."

Besides the temptation to consume what should only be regarded, man is beset by the longing to march toward the unapproachable, which he should be willing merely to look at from afar; and worst of all, he ends by persuading himself that he *has* approached it. "The great error of the Marxists and of all the nineteenth century was to believe that by walking straight ahead one had mounted into the air." What we really want is above us, not ahead of us, and "We cannot take a single step toward heaven. It is not in our power to travel in a vertical direction. If however we look heavenward for a long time, God comes and takes us up." We are free only to change the direction of our glance; we cannot walk into heaven; we cannot rise without being lifted by grace.

The vertical is forbidden to us because the world is the province of gravity and dead weight *(pesanteur)*. The whole universe, as we know it through the senses and the imagination, has been turned over by God to the control of brute mechanism, to necessity and blind force, and that primary physical law by which all things eternally *fall*. The very act of creation entailed the withdrawal of the Creator from the created, so that the sum total of God and his world and all of its creatures is, of course, less than God himself. Having withdrawn from the universe so that it might exist, God is powerless within it, ineffective except as his grace penetrates on special occasions, like a ray of light, the dark mechanical realm of unlimited misery.

Yet we must *love* this world, this absence of God by virtue of which we are, for only through it, like the smile of the beloved through pain, can we sense the perfectly nonpresent Being who alone can redeem it. "In the beauty of the world, brute necessity becomes an object of love. What is more beautiful than the action of gravity on the fugitive folds of the sea waves or on the almost eternal folds of the mountains?"

This world is the only reality available to us, and if we do not love it in all its terror, we are sure to end up loving the "imaginary," our own dreams and self-deceits, the utopias of the politicians, or the futile promises of future reward and consolation which the misled blasphemously call "religion." The soul has a million dodges for protecting itself against the acceptance and love of the emptiness, that "maximum distance between God and God," which is the universe; for the price of such acceptance and love is abysmal misery. And yet it is the only way. "If still persevering in our love, we fall to the point where the soul cannot keep back the cry 'My God, my God, why hast thou forsaken me?' if we remain at this point without ceasing to love, we end by touching something that is not affliction, not joy, something that is the central essence, necessary and pure, something not of the senses, common to joy and sorrow: the very love of God."

The final crown of the life of holiness is the moment of utter despair in which one becomes totally a "slave," naked and abandoned and nailed to the cross in imitation of the absolute spiritual poverty of Christ. "Extreme affliction . . . is a nail whose point is applied at the very center of the soul, whose head is all necessity spreading throughout space and time. . . . He whose soul remains ever turned toward God though pierced with a nail finds himself nailed to the center of the universe . . . at the intersection of creation and its Creator . . . at the intersection of the arms of the Cross."

On the cross, deceit is no longer possible; we are forced to "recognize as real what we would not even have believed possible," and having yielded ourselves in love to spiritual poverty, spiritual nudity, to death itself, even to the point of provisionally renouncing the hope of immortality, we are ready for the final gesture of obedience: the surrender of the last vestiges of selfhood. In the ultimate "nuptial yes," we must de-create our egos, offer up everything we have ever meant by "I," so that the Divine Love may pass unimpeded through the space we once occupied, close again on Itself. "We are created for this consent, and for this alone."

Missoula, Montana
—1951

On Living with Simone Weil

To WRITE about Simone Weil* is an act of engagement terrifying in its implications. I have never hesitated to take up living issues either from the fear of being proved wrong by developing events or out of tenderness toward the vanity and self-deceit of others. Pious footnotes on established reputations have seemed to me as unattractive as retrospective insights into yesterday's causes. But I have never dealt with a personality so painfully and inexhaustibly contemporaneous as Simone Weil; though ten years dead, she remains living in a way that Alger Hiss, for all the resurrection of his name in the press and on the radio, is not. Beside her, the Rosenbergs, McCarthy seem ghosts, less real than what one has written about them. Only she among recent figures with whom I have dealt in print has really *happened* to me, become an event in my life as well as an item in my bibliography; or, to put it more precisely, I have become an event in hers, a minor event in the pathos and comedy of a life which is not yet through.

It is for this reason that I am almost tempted to believe that, given the chance, I would not write on her again. It all seemed innocent enough in the beginning: the brief note from Irving Kristol asking me to read *La pesanteur et la grâce* and to put something down if I felt moved to, my own passionate response to that selection of aphorisms from her notebooks, my first piece on her in *Commentary,* my introduction to *Waiting for God,* and then—the deluge.

---

* Simone Weil, *The Notebooks* (tr. by Arthur Wills), 2 vols.

To this day I am not sure that the day's mail will not bring me a new volume of "mystical" poems, shamelessly turgid and printed at the author's expense; or another letter from Ceylon or Cuba or the Philippines thanking me for my essay and hinting shyly that the writer, too, has had experiences like Simone Weil's. Visiting clergymen in Missoula, Montana, Episcopal or Catholic, will stop in to see me, or intellectual priests exiled in obscure towns in the West send me clippings from parochial magazines.

I have finally the sense of a fragmented, ill-assorted community of admirers of Simone Weil, nuts, lonely neurotics, ex-radicals, existentialists, discontented kids trying to find each other, to tell someone who will listen their love for her. It is more than a little embarrassing sometimes: too many confessions more intimate than one should be asked to share; too many muddled confusions that end equating Simone Weil's terrible, bleak vision with the blurred nature-mysticism of Walt Whitman; too many correspondents who have only read excerpts from my piece in *Time*. And, of course, there is *Time* itself, hot always on the trail of the Latest Thing in Religion from Kierkegaard to the Lubovitcher Rebbe, *Time* in whose pages everything sinks to the dead level of the interesting.

I will not pretend that a first appearance in *Time* (where I made my début flanked by a picture of Simone Weil, uncompromisingly ugly and intent) is easy to take for one brought up on left-wing politics, especially since the twinge of guilt is inevitably balanced by a small flush of pride. But there were favorable responses, too, from Herbert Read and Upton Sinclair—even offers of audiences with the Pope and Sholem Asch, both of which temptations I managed finally to resist; in short, distinguished recognition and some comic relief.

But this is only a part of the picture, in a sense the least fascinating; for at the same moment that a doctor in the Celebes was sitting down to write me a note of appreciation, a professor in the Hebrew University (I am told) was hurling the *Commentary* containing my article through a window. When I tried not long ago to persuade my publisher to include one of my Weil pieces (I *would* still write them, after all) in my collection of essays, I was assured from the friendliest of sources that "everybody" considers these tributes to contemporary sanctity well below my usual standards. It all depends on who your "everybody" is. Certainly, Simone Weil has stirred up—and continues to excite—a resistance whose strength I at first underestimated. Though her flirtation with the Roman Church has never quite satisfied the staunchest guardians of orthodoxy, it has seemed sufficiently compromising to justify hysteria to a certain kind of middle-class mind, for which anti-Catholicism plays the role of anti-Semitism among the lower classes. And my willingness to abide this flirtation has led to a still circulating series of rumors about my own conversion to Catholicism, of which my article seemed in some quarters to be an encoded confession.

I do not want to gloss over the problems of Simone Weil's attitude toward her own Jewishness, which are complex and deserve a treatment equally complex, at which I have made an attempt in my *Commentary* essay. I want to remark here only how various other attitudes are involved with and disguised by the righteous protest against her alleged anti-Semitism. The first of these is a psychoanalytically oriented distrust of such "neurotic symptoms" as the denial of the self and the belief in a direct communion with God—as if supreme goodness were not as likely to look like mental disease as mental health. The second and more important is the desire among those whose former radicalism has shrunk to little besides antireligion to resist the "failure of nerve" and the "return to God." Like color distinctions to the poor whites, it is their last claim to a kind of superiority; and I know now that one must be cautious in hacking away at such a claim as if only principle and truth rather than prestige and self-respect were involved.

In any case, the opposition is formidable, entrenched in the most fashionable tolerance of the moment and even commercially enough of a threat to have scared the publishers of the English translation of *Waiting for God* into expurgating that book. What they removed from the volume in question was a piece, included in the French version, in which Simone Weil retold the myth of Noah's drunkenness to prove that Shem was the evil son, Ham the real chosen of God. I first learned of this bowdlerization when I protested the cutting of a reference to it in my own introductory essay and an editor from Putnam's wrote: "As you know, it has been considerably criticized in Jewish circles. . . ." He went on to assure me that it was being saved for "possible future publication," but it has not, of course, yet appeared. This strikes me, I must confess, as sheer comedy—self-censorship out of the purest commercial motives; but my next adventure was more pathetic, the motives at stake more confused.

There has been going on, since the publishing of Simone Weil's work began, a struggle between her Jewish family and her Catholic literary executors, in which each would like by selection and emphasis to make it clear that at the end of her life she was clearly moving away from or toward the Roman Church. Since I had expressed a view that she would never have become a Catholic because she found too great a "Jewish" element in that church, I had apparently succeeded in offending both, certainly in pleasing neither. At any rate, I found myself in the dead center of a fight, a vulnerable target between two strongly entrenched forces. As a result, my introductory note (which Herbert Read had suggested be published with the British edition of *Lettre à un réligieux* and perhaps translated for appearance in France) was vetoed by her parents. They seem to have been deeply hurt by my view of them as urging against their daughter's ideal of self-immolation the desirability of sustaining one's life in at least minimum security. My description of the absurd conflict between their desire as parents to see Simone happy and her desire to die they read as a reproach to them for pandering to their own comfort. Mme. Weil wrote bitterly of her thankless labors as a housewife, her husband's self-sacrifice as a doctor. To justify myself seemed impossible; but I tried at least to say something of my dismay at having cost them pain—bourgeois father myself and knowing how I could not have resisted wishing for my own child that she *not* achieve sainthood at such a cost; and I welcome the chance to repeat this in print.

No matter—except as I sit over these latest volumes of Simone Weil to appear in America and live again my relationship with her: my role in introducing her to this country (the publisher's canniness I appreciate only now in having a Jew to do the job), my implication with her family and with her mission of spreading the scandal and pain she thought to be the way to God. It is from these journals before me that the selections I first read were chosen, well chosen, for there is little new in the larger work: the same concept of the Void; the same obsessive metaphors of eating and female ugliness; the same desire to substitute for Judaism an Egyptian-Greek beginning for Christianity; the same hatred of war and the state and the self; the same realization that in our age the nonbeliever may be closer to a knowledge of God than the pious communicant. All that is added is a further sense of the hash of incomplete projects and half-completed syntheses out of which Simone Weil's aphorisms were extracted; of the sometimes nearly incoherent jumble of mathematics and comparative mythology, politics, and bodily pain against which she defined her vision. It is a true vision all the same: a vision capable still of giving offense and illumination; testimony to a life no one would dare wish for his child or pray for himself, but which he is proud to know was lived in his time by one who fought for causes that he, too, dreamed, and who was like him (whatever the word finally means) a Jew.

—1957

THREE

Straddling the Wall

THE WALL, we are told in an "Editor's Prologue," is actually the work of a certain Noach Levinson, Archivist of the Warsaw Ghetto, whose collection of documents and notes on Jewish life in the days of the destruction was dug up from its hiding place just after the war; "the Editor" has merely cut and arranged items from the collection. But a note on the back of the title page warns us that the "archive" is merely a hoax, and the book jacket assures us that we are reading a novel by John Hersey—presumably on the principle that there is no use taking chances and that more people are likely to read novels than histories. And what of the misguided reader who avoids the blurbs on book jackets? After all, there *was* a Warsaw Ghetto, and everyone knows that Hersey's book on Hiroshima was non-fiction, and therefore. . . . A further note adds to the confusion, asserting that "the substance is history" but that "the details are invented." Why so elaborate a pretense of subterfuge?

If *The Wall* gains anything from all this machinery, it does not gain enough to make a difference; for it remains on the whole a dull and unconvincing novel. Given its subject, before which the private imagination falters and the public imagination takes refuge in rhetoric, the unconvincingness is expected, perhaps inevitable; but the dullness demands a special talent. Indeed, that dullness is, in a sense, deliberate, the product of the very good sense and good taste that here and there win for Mr. Hersey some local successes. There is practically none of the overwriting one might look for in connection with such a theme; and any sentimentality that creeps in is reasonably quiet and well-behaved. There is, too, a solid core of carefully accumulated fact that is impressive, though never moving, beneath the conscientious underwriting.

Within the book's well-bred American limitations, the East European Jews it pretends to evoke are stifled; when they momentarily materialize, we catch them squirming. One has the impression of a Gentile with good intentions retelling a Yiddish story but avoiding the extreme intonations that make the point—in order to keep from giving offense. The language of the protagonists suffers especially; what there is in Yiddish of the richly vulgar, the outrageously exaggerated, has almost disappeared. It is typical that one characteristically gross idiom which slips by Mr. Hersey's guard is expurgated in translation, *"Geh, kak' oif'm yam"* becoming "Go use the ocean for a toilet seat."

In its attempt to seem merely the jottings of an archivist the book succeeds in being, in the Jamesean sense, scarcely *written* at all. Avoiding the poetic tone, the epic ambition, it is drawn toward the low-keyed prose of the report. Stylistically, it exists at the point where history, journalism, and fiction blur into that un-form which we may as well call, as the movies have taught us to, the "documentary." Overwhelmed, perhaps, by the political fact which was his occasion, Hersey does not dare to give the demands of form precedence over those of documentation; and yet he is no longer content to do the modest job of reportage that made *Hiroshima* effective. In the end, he merely flirts with fiction: sketching characters, tentatively striving for inwardness, but always retreating to the "facts" of the researcher.

The dry, matter-of-fact approach of the reporter is viable in literature only when, as in Defoe or Swift, the fable is not "true," but merely the outward form of a consistent and serious symbolism trying to get by in a literal-minded age. In Hersey's book, the opposite is the case; his book is an allegory stood on its head, with its literal story being verified history but its inner meanings essentially false. What one resents is *The Wall*'s effort to bully us into accepting moral and political insights that we know are invalid by insisting on the documentary veracity of a historical event that we cannot deny. As a result, we are left feeling that the value of the book depends entirely on the truth of its statements down to their last detail; the whole structure, we suspect, would collapse if it turned out

that in Warsaw during the March of 1941 there were not 1,668 but
1,669 deaths from typhus.

How different this is from what may properly be considered a
novel we can see by reminding ourselves of the opening of Kafka's
Amerika, in which the very "mistake" of placing a sword in the
hand of the Statue of Liberty assures us that the book we are beginning is not less but more true than a document. When a writer com-
pels us outward toward the world of statistics, he betrays a basic
uncertainty about his ability to convey poetic conviction and inward
truth, which can lead him only into further difficulty and confusion.
To maintain the kind of verisimilitude he has chosen, Hersey is
forced to impose unnecessary strains on our credulity. Wishing his
account to seem more archive than fiction, Hersey narrates it all
from the point of view of the single archivist Levinson; but to make
this probable, he asks us to believe that scores of people have chosen to confess to one man their most intimate thoughts and have
recollected, while doing so, the most insignificant details of their
past. The author himself feels the absurdity of this from time to
time and apologizes in a backhand way, putting into the mouth of
Levinson the reader's objections. "Why does she remember, and
why does she feel that she has to tell me, a detail like that?" "He
spoke to me as an ear, not as a man."

But the most palpable piece of stage-managing required by
Hersey's machinery comes in the final scene, the theatrical *finale* in
which a handful of survivors crouch in a sewer just outside the wall
of the burning Ghetto, and Levinson *interviews* them: a *Time* reporter on the spot or a Gallup Poll man taking notes. "Some of my
friends have mentioned seeing a change in you during recent
months. Have you felt such a change. . . . Could you describe this
change? Why this change?" And they all, in excrement halfway to
their knees, dutifully answer. It is a picture not only of the Warsaw
Ghetto, but of a world we continue to inhabit, trapped between the
crap and the well-intentioned inquisitors.

This, of course, Hersey does not know, being aware only that
his quizzees must (even as we must) answer so that his charade can
end on a note of hope. To symbolize that hope, *Hatikvah* is played
offstage on the concertina of a doomed man, even as Hersey's protagonists make their affirmations like the convicted defendants in a

Soviet trial. If he had been content merely to aim at a good book, he might have avoided such embarrassments; but he is driven by the desire to write a *great* one, a work of art as great as its subject. In the interest of such greatness, he feels obliged to go beyond the mere evocation of horror and despair and defeat, feels compelled to demonstrate that the ordeal of the Ghetto was, for a chosen few at least, a school for nobility. It is possible that this was, in fact, true; but for a writer to convince us of it is another matter. In this regard, Hersey's plight is rather like that of an author who has imagined a great poet as his protagonist and finds himself forced to invent verses capable of persuading us of his protagonist's talent. So Mr. Hersey must persuade us that his ennobled survivors are, indeed, noble; and to do this, he must find for them a language appropriate to their redeemed state rather than to the editorial demands of the *New Yorker*.

Realizing the difficulty of this, he seeks refuge at first in quotation, putting in the mouth of his archivist certain phrases from the eminent Jewish writer Peretz. When the German flamethrowers have driven the last Jewish resisters underground, we are permitted to listen to Levinson addressing a gathering in an airless bunker. He speaks to his comrades of Peretz, rehearsing for them the remembered words of that dead author.

> Now I am not advocating that we shut ourselves up in a spiritual ghetto. On the contrary, we should get out of such a ghetto. But we should get out as Jews, with our own spiritual treasures. We should interchange, give and take, but not beg.
>
> Ghetto is impotence. Cultural cross-fertilization is the only possibility for human development. Humanity must be the synthesis, the sum, the quintessence of all national cultural forms and philosophies.

As rhetoric this is not disgraceful, but as relevant wisdom it is of doubtful worth. Peretz was dead before even the first of the World Wars was over; and repeated after the final outbreak of terror, his phrases seem old-fashioned, inadequate with their proffered hope of cultural assimilation and a commonwealth of enlightened men. This was the battered hope men carried still in their hearts before Warsaw and the concentration camps; but with what was it replaced? This question, too, Levinson-Hersey tries to answer, listing one by one, as in a morality play, the partial answers of the handful left in the sewers to confront their inevitable death.

First the Zionist speaks ("the Jewish ethical tradition is worth preserving—it is the basis of all Western monotheism, after all . . . and the best way of preserving it is to give it a home"), then the Socialist ("Judge me, Levinson. Have I or have I not tried to put human understanding into my politics. . ."), then Rachel Apt, heroine of the tale, and representative of a modern religiosity without religion ("I am rather unclear as to God. But so far as the rest of religion is concerned, I think there is only one thing: not to hurt anybody"). It is a crescendo of clichés which it seems impossible to augment; but Levinson has already outdone the hoariest of them, declaring: "I think we are indeed involved in the struggle of Humanity against Anti-Humanity. Here, we are outnumbered. We are a little hysterical. We may all die. But we will win." The Zionist, the Socialist, the Jewish Heroine, the subtle Scholar among them can do no better; and, indeed, the final condemnation of the book is that we are prepared to believe that out of the mouths of Hersey's characters precisely such platitudes would come: after the Terror, such pious banalities. Poor Jews!

—1950

Partisan Review: Phoenix or Dodo?

I CANNOT WRITE about the *Partisan Review* objectively and coolly. In dealing with it, I have the sense of beginning my own autobiography, or, more precisely, of treating that part of my life which is typical rather than peculiar: my life as an urban American Jew, who came of age intellectually during the Depression: who discovered Europe for the imagination before America: who was influenced by Marxist ideas, Communist and Trotskyist; who wanted desperately to feel that the struggle for a revolutionary politics and the highest literary standards was a single struggle (but who had more and more trouble believing it as the years went on); whose political certainty unraveled during the second World War. . . I forget after a while whether I am writing about myself and my friends or about the magazine we used to fight for and argue over in 1937 and '38 and '39. I do not mean we *liked* it, then—far from it! Every issue seemed to us to fail some large, abstract notion of *Partisan Review*-ness, some ideal, it now seems clear to me, of ourselves. No sooner was *Partisan* a year old than this year's level seemed to us a vast falling off from the year before. The point is, of course, that what is merely typical of oneself is bound to appear comic, embarrassing, depressing and a bore; and yet—I remember K., now the author of two novels, one of whose first ambitious pieces of fiction was a parody of a *Partisan Review* story we all mailed off together as a huge joke, but who, ten years later, was publishing regularly in *PR*. I remember my own sense of being misrepresented when I, in turn, began to appear in its pages; and my special horror when, after only three contributions, I was mentioned in two separate attacks on *Partisan* as representative of its intellectual vices.

By now I have come a long way from the pattern of my past: a Professor of English Literature, improbably asked for letters of recommendation by aspiring students; a father of six children, who lives over five hundred miles from the nearest big city and is surrounded by those who, if they know *Partisan* at all, have picked it up in a university library rather than off the "literature table" of a deviationist Marxist sect. Yet I have accepted my fate with all its contradictions: I stand somehow for *PR* and *PR* for me; I do not like it, but I cannot deny it. I know that even my feeling of being misrepresented is typical, as is my lack of love for the magazine. It is not a publication one loves; only its enemies are passionate. Nor does *PR* love its own children; I am aware that at the very moment I am losing a good academic job because I have appeared too often on its pages (and am therefore obviously "negative" as well as Jewish), *PR* is preparing to blast me publicly for believing in God. This strikes me as reasonably just as well as amusing—as amusing almost as the letter I had not long ago from a writer who is perhaps the best of the younger American novelists. "As for *PR*," he writes, "you know I never took that dodo for a phoenix. . . ." We both remember, of course, that it was *Partisan* which almost alone published him in the days when he was fighting to establish his reputation; but his comment is also just and a joke and part of the history of the magazine.

The real riddle of *Partisan Review* has always seemed to me the question of how the mouthpiece of so small and special a group as I have been defining (I should be much more surprised to discover that I am a "typical American" than that I am a typical *Partisan* writer) has managed to become the best-known serious magazine in America, and certainly, of all American magazines with intellectual ambitions, the one most read in Europe. That these are facts, I think there can be no doubt; at least, they are invariably mentioned with horror in anti-*Partisan* tirades. For better or for worse, *PR* has come to symbolize highbrow literature in America, and to suffer the twin indignities of the highbrow in our world: to be despised without understanding, and to be taken up by the culturally fashionable in equal ignorance.

Two examples, picked at random out of many, may serve to make the point. In a recent article, a certain reputable professor of American Literature sought to make clear his contempt for the politics of Mark Twain by writing, "We know this type well: the liberal who is not the tough realist. . . . You will find him vending his misanthropy in the *Partisan Review*." The reputable professor feels free to assume that there will be no doubt among academic readers about the meaning of his allusion. But the symbol is effective in Hollywood as well as at Princeton or Harvard. A couple of years ago, I paid a brief visit to an acquaintance who had been translated from an editorship in a publishing house to the position of a movie producer; and I found him in the midst of the appropriate splendor: white rugs on the floor, ponies for each of his children—and in the middle of a large, free-form cocktail table—a single copy of *PR*—to show, I suppose, that he was not yet lost to intellectual respectability.

Not only the purveyors of culture, however, high and low, accept this equation of *Partisan* and highbrow; it holds water for people who have never even seen the periodical, perhaps have never known one of its readers in their lives. It is, as a matter of fact, by no means easy to meet such readers. In its nearly twenty years of history, *PR* has never claimed more than ten thousand subscribers, and probably has considerably fewer at the present moment; and yet it is referred to in such mass-circulation journals as *Life* and *Time* with perfect confidence that it will stir the proper responses in their vast audience. Most of its subscribers have, to be sure, clustered about the two great cities of New York and Chicago (44%, according to a poll taken one year by the editors); and New York, at least, has been traditionally the taste-making center of the nation.

Besides, the split among the various kinds of art in America and their appropriate audiences into low, middle, and high has surrendered the creation, consumption, and judgment of serious literature into the hands of the very few. It is against those few that *Partisan's* five to ten thousand faithful must be measured, and not against the 160,000,000 of the latest census figures. In that relatively restricted group, the thirties were marked by a turning away from the hinterland of America to Europe in a search for literary materials and examples. In that constant turning from East to West to East which characterizes our culture, the vanes pointed East once more; and no one seemed better suited for mediating between Europe and America than the kind of second generation Jew who in America's big cities was trying to find his own identity in the pages of *transition* and Karl Marx's *Capital*. Certainly, the Jews were the only immigrant group that had brought with it a considerable Old World culture to which it clung, refusing to cast it into the melting pot with the same abandon with which southern European or Scandinavian peasants were willing to toss away their few scraps of European spiritual goods.

It was the sons of the original Jewish immigrants, disabused of the legend of a Golden America by the Great Depression and attracted toward the Communist Party, who formed the core of the John Reed Club of New York which first sponsored the *Partisan Review*. In a handful of American cities, such "cultural" organizations, controlled by the Communists and called after native American radicals like John Reed or Jack London, flourished in the late thirties—as part of a strategy aimed at capturing the prestige of the "intellectuals" for the cause of the Soviet Union. It is important to remember that *PR* was born of such a marriage of Greenwich Village and Marxism—or more properly, from the attempt to woo the disaffected, rootless American, who wandered into New York in search of cultural freedom, from Bohemianism to Radicalism.

Partisan Review in its present form, however, begins with a declaration of independence from the orthodox Communists who ordained its beginnings. Its emergence as an independent journal is one symptom among many of the growing uneasiness of a certain segment of American writers, whom the Depression and the Spanish Civil War had persuaded into a temporary alliance with the Communist Party. From 1937 on (the new *PR* appeared first in the fall of that year), the Communists in America lost more and more of their respectable, intellectual fellow-travelers—indeed, almost deliberately jettisoned them for movie stars, script writers, and authors of detective stories as the Popular Front reached its peak of development. Into the cultural vacuum thus created, moved the *Partisan Review*. It was for many a transition from "revolutionary art" back to old-style "aestheticism" or forward to middle-class accommodation (though of this they were not then aware): for others merely the way into a lonelier and lonelier non-conformism.

From the Communists, the new periodical inherited, first of all, a name (at one point later on, when no one was any longer clear exactly what they were "partisan" *for*—there was an unsuccessful attempt to change that name); second, two editors: Philip Rahv and William Phillips, who alone have remained with the publication through countless editorial shifts, thus giving the magazine what continuing character it has; and third, a certain kind of bad manners, traditional in the Marxist movement. There is a polemical vigor and toughness about *PR* which has survived almost all its causes; occasionally that toughness hardens into a pose, but it is always a safeguard against stuffiness and gentility. Born into a dispute (thirty days after its inception, its editors were already labeled by their old comrades "slanderers of the working class . . . turncoats . . . agents provocateurs . . . strikebreakers!" and they were returning abuse for abuse), it has continued to ignore the rules of gentlemanly debate. Often when its collaborators have no one else to attack, they gouge and kick each other like marines stirred up to fight among themselves, just to keep their hands in. Though its founding fathers tend more and more to show their old scars rather than risk getting new ones, they have remained old soap-boxers, which for me, at least, seems preferable to the young academicians or genteel undergraduate admirers of Wyndham Lewis who are found, for example, in *The Hudson Review*. Of all American magazines of discussion, only *Partisan* can be said never to talk to itself; to a few, yes, or to a crowd expected in advance to be hostile—but that is something else again.

There were two motives which impelled the editors of the new *PR* to break from the domination of the Communist Party: first, a desire for cultural autonomy, a feeling that orthodox Stalinism was hedging literature about with the "zeal of vigilantes"; and second, political disagreements of a Trotskyist hue with the official Communist line. Both led to long-term difficulties that have helped determine the nature of the magazine. From their second motive, the editors of *PR* (though most of them did not in fact ever become official Trotskyites) inherited a minor but troublesome vice: an obsessive anti-Stalinism and a myopic concern with sectarian Marxist politics, that, especially in the earlier years, hedged the magazine about with a technical jargon and the sort of parochial fervor which baffles and bores an outsider. After a while, even the insiders, who were not of the sternest, began to wilt at the prospect of yet another scholastic debate on the nature of the Soviet State.

From the first motive, *PR* inherited a whole Chinese nest of interlocking questions, which they have never solved theoretically but which their whole career has been an attempt to answer in practice. If one really believes (as *PR* declared in an early manifesto) that "the tradition of aestheticism" is dead or ought to be and that literature finds its "final justification" in the "historic process," how can one avoid setting political standards for art and eventually harrying the artist precisely as the Communists have done? This is an especially acute problem if one's approach to the "historic process" is revolutionary or even liberal; for it is a baffling fact of our time that many contemporary artists of the first rank are politically reactionary, as in the cases of Yeats, Eliot, Pound, Lawrence, etc. Does one print the work of such misguided writers for the sake of some presumed independent aesthetic value? And how can such values exist if works of art are really rooted in history?

The *de facto* answer of *PR* has been to print Allen Tate, T. S. Eliot, and other artists whose politics it abhors. For a while, indeed, it was the chief American outlet for Eliot, not only his poetry but even an occasional essay on social matters; and as time went on, certain old standbys like James T. Farrell seemed actually to be pushed aside in favor of defter though less "revolutionary" authors, especially those enjoying critical acclaim. What lay behind such a strategy? Unkind critics accused *PR* of institutionalizing schizophrenia; unkinder ones insisted that its editors were shamelessly pursuing "big names."

The truth is, I think, that *PR* has been obsessed with the notion of a two-fold *avant-garde,* political and artistic, both segments regarded as a threat by middle-class philistines. Since the magazine actually came into being at the end of a period rather than a beginning, at the moment when experimentalism in art was being consolidated and academicized all over the world, the concept that serious art is, *per se,* as revolutionary as Marxism has been difficult to maintain. It has been somewhat easier to foster that illusion in respect to painting by espousing the newer versions of abstractionism, or in music, with a spirited apology for the twelve-tone row, than to sustain it in defense of these newer writers, who (aside from such "standards" as Eliot) have been the actual official favorites of *PR:* Malraux, Silone, Koestler, Sartre, Moravia, or George Orwell, to whom *Partisan* once awarded a one thousand dollar literary prize. Ideologically, these writers may represent progressive trends; but technically, they are not very interesting, ranging from glib traditionalism to simple ineptness; and in Orwell's case actually being on record against "advanced" art. Just as *PR* comes into existence at the instant of the liquidation of revolutionary politics as a force in American intellectual life, so it presides (quite unconsciously at first) over the liquidation of experimentalism in art. This has irked various defenders of post-World War I "new literature," ranging from Parker Tyler to Paul Goodman to Harold Rosenberg, men who began as collaborators of the magazine but have one by one withdrawn from its pages. Rosenberg has written a valedictory attack on what *Partisan* has become, dubbing its present writers a "herd of independent minds" and treating them as enemies of serious art.

Despite the fact that *PR*'s notions of an *avant-garde* reach nostalgically back to the very twenties whose values it betrays, those notions have helped develop one of its most valuable features: a series of acute exposés of certain highly regarded writers who pander to the timid, cheery bourgeois mind, which, even after fifty years, persists in the belief that the aging purveyors of the "new literature" (even Eliot!) somehow subvert morality and patriotism. The second World War brought to America a peculiarly violent recrudescence of this attitude; philistine apologists like Archibald MacLeish cried out that the antiwar, antisentimental nature of our literature in the twenties and thirties had left us powerless in the forties to combat Fascism, while Van Wyck Brooks was insisting that the "secondary" literature of Joyce or Proust or Eliot had all along been an offense to the human spirit.

Dwight Macdonald in an essay called *Kulturbolschewismus* and M. D. Zabel in *The Poet on Capitol Hill* demonstrated with wit and passion how such arguments, proposed in the name of American democracy, actually represent totalitarian impulses, paralleling the attacks on the arts of Germany and Russia. In the atmosphere of controversy and self-congratulation which surrounded these two pieces, the editors were able to defend their previous principles of selection against the charges of contradictoriness by declaring, "It is coming to be something of a revolutionary act simply to print serious creative writing." When the culture-censors ten years later closed in on Ezra Pound, who had been awarded a coveted literary prize, *Partisan*'s editors, troubled by his anti-Semitism, were no longer so certain where their hearts lay; but in 1941 they were courageous and unequivocal.

Our entry into the war followed hard on these polemics, bringing a crisis in the history of *Partisan Review*. The editors found themselves not only confused but not even sharing a common confusion about the attitude to take toward our participation in the fight against Hitler. Dwight Macdonald, who had played a leading editorial role in the years just before Pearl Harbor and was still maintaining the traditional revolutionary position (the defeat of Hitler could only be forwarded by a redoubled struggle for socialism in the United States), left the board of editors; and with his going the magazine came to take political stands on specific issues less and less often. McCarthyism for a little while stirred it to specific political discussion and forced the resignation of the most right-wing of its long-time associates, James Burnham; but in general *PR* tended more and more to invest its post-Marxian zeal in considering broadly defined problems of American culture. The clash of High Brow and Low Brow has gradually usurped the place of Class War in its working mythology.

The editors have moved since variously toward skepticism, New Dealism and non-Marxian socialism; and though occasionally a cry is raised in its columns against the "Age of Conformism," most of its collaborators have been able to imagine no formulation of their plight which transcends the dilemma of adapting to current American life or sighing for the good old revolutionary days. Yet despite all changes, *PR* has remained in tone and tactics different from other American magazines of its category: the only periodical in our intellectual community for which politics in the European sense (something beyond choosing between Democrats and Republicans on set occasions) has ever existed. That old political passion survives in two forms: in the conviction that art is rooted in society, however one understands that society, and must be discussed in terms of those roots; and in a stubborn secularism which has outlived the revolutionary beliefs which once sustained it. From Edmund Wilson to Lionel Trilling, the most characteristic critical voice of *PR* has attempted to assert the sociological thesis against an evergrowing tendency toward intrinsic or "pure" textual criticism, and has sought to defend it against its profanation by the Stalinist or liberaloid theory that art must embody "progressive" ideas.

Occasionally in reading *Partisan* these days one has the sense of a weary but gallant voice crying, "Rosinante to the road again," as the editors print the replies to their latest questionnaire on the Return to Religion. When they reconsider their other long-time favorite problem: the Relation of the Intellectual to American Culture, they cannot help being aware of how far they have come since, say, Dreiser's offhand dismissal of official "Americanism" in the earliest of their symposia. But when it is a matter of "the retreat to faith," the old forces rally round and the majority opinion, naturalist and "scientific," rings out loud and clear, as if nothing had happened in twenty years—and we were all rebels still—with no income tax returns to trouble us.

In 1950, a symposium on "Religion and the Intellectuals" took up where an earlier discussion labeled "The New Failure of Nerve" had left off seven years before; but whereas in the earlier forum, part at least of *Partisan*'s fervor was directed against doctrinaire Marxism, this time the Marxist issue was left far out on the periphery. The finish of the first Symposium had found Professor Sidney Hook (who is almost the official spokesman for *PR* in these matters) closed in argument with an orthodox Socialist; the close of the second found the same Professor Hook grappling with a slippery Christian apologist, Ernest van den Haag. Hook has always struck me as a brilliant though cruel polemicist and a courageous man, but his views on religion are vitiated by the fact that he can, apparently, never really credit the fact that anyone actually believes in God. His attitude in this regard is like that of an uninitiated small boy toward sex: he has heard of it, and he pretends to give credence to its reality, but that papa and mama really *do* it is unthinkable!

It remains further to be said that its origin in the Village-Marxist atmosphere of New York has influenced *PR* in two other significant ways: leaving it peculiarly "European" and resolutely anti-"academic." Its European flavor is partly a matter of the taste of its editors; its favorite literary ancestors are Dostoevsky and Tolstoi; its favorite moderns, Malraux, Koestler, Silone, Kafka, Musil, Sartre, Moravia, etc; and translations of their works will frequently be the only imaginative literature in a given issue. Even more characteristic, perhaps, are those communications from European cultural centers, which lend much of its peculiar tone to *PR:* the Paris letters of H. J. Kaplan and Nicola Chiaramonte, as well as the Italian letters of the latter and the London letters by Koestler and Orwell (attempts to institute similar regular communications from American centers away from New York have always stuttered out to nothing) have kept *Partisan*'s readers in touch not only with the literary and political news but with the very gossip of Europe—a narrow and sometimes *chic* Europe, to be sure, but a real one. The *PR* reader has, by virtue of these letters, always felt a good deal closer to Paris than to, say, Missoula, Montana; and though there is something a little absurd about this, there is also something valuable. *PR* has kept open a dialogue between our writers and certain writers on the continent; and it alone has been able to do this because it alone among our periodicals has been interested in and articulate about those "general ideas," with which the continental mind engages so passionately but which most Americans notoriously ignore in favor of documented facts or textual analysis. The most famous of these general ideas is the somewhat ambiguous one of "alienation": a concept which joins together the Marxist beginnings of *PR* with its early leanings toward depth psychology and its later interest in existentialism.

The belief in the "alienation" of the writer and intellectual from the community in a time of decaying values has seemed to certain of its critics to obsess the *Partisan Review,* and to lend a characteristic note of melancholy to its fiction and poetry as well as to its more ideological pieces. Protests have rung out from the beginning against the mixture of self-pity and bravado implicit in this view of the writer at odds with his world; and just lately, for instance, the editor of a provincial little magazine has described it as an "attitude which seems to come from reading *The Golden Bowl* on the B.M.T. subway." In one sense, such a view is indeed a peculiarity, almost a disease of the social group out of which *Partisan* comes: a development of the special sense of loneliness of the city-dweller, the Jew, the Marxist in an un-Marxist America—and especially of the left-wing Communist cut off even from the comforting sense of solidarity with the Soviet Union and "right-minded" liberalism. On the other hand, it is the traditional European view of the artist in America from Baudelaire on Poe to D. H. Lawrence on the classic American authors; and as mass culture advances throughout the Western world, it comes to describe the plight of the artist everywhere. It is true enough that "alienation" has sometimes been celebrated by *PR,* rather than explored; but on the other hand, its writers have done more than any others I know to describe the situation of a minority high culture in a mass society committed to the majoritarian principle.

In its earliest manifesto, *PR* declared its defiance of all "academicians from the University"; and it has continued its rather harried financial existence via "angels" and begging letters—but always without the sponsorship of any educational institution.[1] This has been especially difficult in America, where the intellectual and his pursuits are granted full recognition and status only when they are associated with "higher education" and the universities have stood almost alone in subsidizing serious magazines. Even the Rockefeller Foundation, which in recent years has given support of one kind or another to such ventures, has invested only in periodicals whose respectability was already insured by an institutional connection, *Kenyon Review, Sewanee Review,* etc. *Partisan* has accordingly remained quite different in tone from those magazines that have defined themselves against the tendencies of old-line literary scholarship and whose *raison d'être* has been the struggle to reform the teaching of literature in the college classroom. *PR*'s ideo-

---

[1] In 1963, Richard Poirier, Chairman of the English Department at Rutgers University, became chief editor of *Partisan Review,* and William Phillips, one of its founders, was made a professor at the same institution. Since then it has largely been supported by that institution; but to what degree this represents a change in *Partisan Review* and to what degree one in the American university is the subject for another article which I am resolved never to write.

logical center has never become (no matter how many professors it lists among its contributors) the argument between the "New Critics" and the "Old Scholars," that is, a debate about pedagogy. It arises rather from that strange mingling of malicious gossip and disinterested argument about ideas that characterizes a social evening in New York. What the café is for Europe, such parties are for America—and it is out of them that *Partisan* has drawn its reigning concerns and its tone.

There are certain obvious limitations implicit in originating in so tight and isolated a world; obviously, personalities will play too large a part in any magazine nurtured by that milieu. Marriages and divorces, the falling out with an old mistress or the acquiring of a new one may end by influencing a political manifesto or the review of a new novel. Even the fiction of *PR* tends inevitably toward the *roman à clef,* its contributors feeding on each other like a mutual benefit association of cannibals. And the final absurdity (which I am not inventing but reporting) is the *PR* writer who produces a novel pillorying another *PR* writer (thinly disguised) for having in a previous book portrayed too bitterly still another *PR* contributor.

Moreover, the editors, to whom the literary cocktail party has been not only a source of images and ideas but also a university, end up without the protection of a traditionally acquired education —and are helplessly jostled by fad and fashion in a frantic drive to keep up with the latest thing. A critic of *PR* writing in 1949 could quite justly observe that up until that time, the magazine had never printed any full-scale article on a literary figure who flourished earlier than the latter half of the nineteenth century. This is, I think, an inevitable consequence of the scrappy, disordered, and largely contemporary culture out of which *PR* is improvised; it is a big price to pay for avoiding the curse of "academicism."

Yet certain qualifications must be made to these more general charges. On the one hand, *Partisan* has always included among its key contributors such generally cultured men as Edmund Wilson; and on the other hand, the American universities have undergone a revolutionary change since 1937 so that the sort of writer who once would have free-lanced out of some big city Bohemia ends up at Iowa State or North Carolina College for Women; and consequently, there has been an inevitable rapprochement between *PR* and what it likes to call "the academy." Not only have professors become its contributors, but its contributors have become professors. The last few years have seen an odd sort of united front between *PR* and *Kenyon Review*,[2] the best of the academic-New Critical quarterlies, whose editor, John Crowe Ransom, not only writes for *Partisan* but has enlisted two of its editors, Rahv himself and Delmore Schwartz, to serve with him in the "School of Letters," a Rockefeller sponsored set-up which grants an M.A. in literature.

Besides, there has always been a loose, hard-to-define but nonetheless real connection between *PR* and Columbia University, which, trapped in the midst of New York City and fed by the subways, manages to be in certain important respects the least academic of academies. Since the death of the old Village and the institutionalization of the American writer, Columbia has come more and more to serve as a kind of intellectual center for the city and consequently for the New York-oriented throughout the nation. *Partisan Review* represents, in the light of this, one more colonizing attempt on the part of a university which has also made its influence felt decisively in such ventures as Readers' Subscription (the highbrow book club of the United States), and Anchor Books, whose distribution of serious, large format books in paper binding has revolutionized American publishing. Among the editors of *Partisan Review,* there have always been professors from Columbia like F. W. Dupee and Lionel Trilling; and in the list of *PR*'s regular contributors still others play a large part, including Meyer Shapiro, whose shadowy but enormous reputation among New York intellectuals as a polymath and whose formative influence on many of those intellectuals cannot be assessed in terms of his relatively limited publication. Lionel Trilling is, of course, the most interesting and influential of the group; much of his criticism has appeared in *PR,* as well as the two short stories which made him a reputation as a fictionist; yet he manages to preserve a remarkable aura of respectability not granted any of his colleagues. Those who condemn all else about the magazine, specifically exempt him from the gen-

---

[2] Just a year or two ago *Kenyon Review* was officially buried, after having dragged out a kind of posthumous half-life for a long time; and its last fiction editor is now filling the same post on *Playboy.*

eral blame; yet he is in most ways not untypical: Jewish, a New Yorker who refuses to leave that city, an exploiter of the themes of anguish and alienation, a naturalist searching for tragedy. But in him the ordinarily annoying pose is mitigated by a soft-spoken style which is modesty itself—and combined with the stance of a nineteenth-century English gentleman-dissenter to produce a version of the *PR* writer as a belated Matthew Arnold.

Whereas Trilling embodies and modifies, in a secondary way, the *PR* spirit, another Columbia figure has presided over the very definition of that spirit: the figure of the eminent philosopher John Dewey, who himself wrote occasionally for *PR,* but whose influence has made itself felt even more effectively through his disciples, Ernest Nagel and Sidney Hook. As a matter of fact, it is the Naturalism of the Columbia school that has outlasted the collapse of its Marxism and that shores up the secularist tough-mindedness of *Partisan Review. PR* was, as one might expect, attracted for a while to the French version of Existentialism. Its atheism, its attempt to find a non-Marxian basis for the revolutionary attitude, its early defiance of Stalinism—all these seemed especially sympathetic to the *Partisan Review* mind. William Barrett, a former professor of philosophy, who finally filled the editorial vacuum left by the resignation of Dwight Macdonald, led the enthusiastic acclaim of Sartre, who threatened for a while to stand permanently in the niche left empty for *PR* by the fall of Karl Marx. But there was something too hasty and *willed* about this allegiance, which has in the last couple of years been struggling vainly to survive the personal encounter of *PR*'s editor with the representatives of Sartrean philosophy. No, Existentialism was for *PR* only an adventure, an affair; their true love has waited patiently for them at home: the spirit of John Dewey. In an unexpected way this alienated, Europe-oriented periodical comes to rest with the most "American" of philosophical systems: the same Deweyan pragmatism which, on another front, has nurtured the progressive educationist. It is a final irony.

What then shall I say at last of *Partisan* and the piece of myself which it represents? After scanning nearly twenty years' worth of it all at once, I feel bound to report that I have felt it to be frequently pontifical and boring, occasionally ritualistic in its repetition of a few sacred themes, generally depressing in the sense it gives of the narrowing down and drying up of political adventurousness and aesthetic experimentalism. I have found its symposia heavy-handed and its culture spotty. I have been appalled by its genuflecting to big names, amused by its occasional compensatory indulgences in the grayest sort of Germanic scholarship, exasperated by its over-adulation of Silone; and at one point I found myself muttering that if I came across the name of Kafka or Jean-Paul Sartre once more I would burn the whole damned pile of back issues. I have been provoked by the number of its contributors, who, having no apparent love for literature, deal with it like a subject they have drawn at random out of a hat; and I have turned away in disgust from certain young operators who by learning to say "milieu" and "situation" have imposed themselves on the editors.

Yet I cannot despise a magazine which has never been afraid of ideas or paralyzed by worries about "good taste"; which has served as a bridge between Europe and America, the free lance and the university; which above all has printed, often before anyone else, such writers of fiction as Saul Bellow, Mary McCarthy, Lionel Trilling, and Delmore Schwartz, such poets as Randall Jarrell, Robert Lowell, and John Berryman, such critics as Edmund Wilson and Lionel Trilling. It is a strange enough bird, the *Partisan Review,* a scraggier, shabbier, more raucous phoenix than we might have hoped for, and one not above crying out its own name at the top of its voice; but it is our only real contender for the title. Blasted into ashes by its enemies, mourned prematurely by its friends, despaired of by its own editors—it yet somehow survives; and that is, after all, the point.

Missoula, Montana
—1956

Saul Bellow

WITH THE PUBLICATION of *Seize the Day,* Saul Bellow has become not merely a writer with whom it is possible to come to terms, but one with whom it is *necessary* to come to terms—perhaps of all our novelists the one we need most to understand if we are to understand what the novel is doing at the present moment. Bellow has endured the almost ritual indignities of the beginning fictionist: his first novel a little over-admired and read by scarcely anyone; his second novel once more critically acclaimed, though without quite the thrill of discovery, and still almost ignored by the larger public; his third novel, thick, popular, reprinted in the paperbacks and somewhat resented by the first discoverers, who hate seeing what was exclusively theirs pass into the public domain; and now a fourth book: a collection of stories, most of which have appeared earlier, a play, and a new novella.

Suddenly, the novelist whom we have not ceased calling a "young writer" (it is a habit hard to break and the final indignity) is established and forty, a part of our lives and something for the really young to define themselves against. But it has become clear that he will continue to write, that he is not merely the author of a novel or two, but a *novelist;* and this in itself is a triumph, a rarity in recent American literary history and especially among the writers with whom we associate Bellow. We think of the whole line of Jewish-American novelists, so like him in origin and aspiration, of Daniel Fuchs and Henry Roth and Nathanael West, those poets and annalists of the thirties who did not survive their age, succumbing to death or Hollywood or a sheer exhaustion of spirit and subject. Or we think of Bellow's own contemporaries, the *Partisan Review* group, urban Jews growing up under the threat of failure and terror, the Depression and Spain and the hopelessly foreseen coming of war. We remember, perhaps, Isaac Rosenfeld or H. J. Kaplan or Oscar Tarcov or Delmore Schwartz or even Lionel Trilling, who had also to be twice born, committed first to Stalinism and then to disenchantment, but who were capable of using imaginatively only the disenchantment. And remembering these, we recall beginnings not quite fulfilled, achievements which somehow betrayed initial promises. Certain short stories remain in our minds (flanked by all those essays, those explanations and rejoinders and demonstrations of wit): Kaplan's "The Mohammedans," Rosenfeld's "The Pyramids," Schwartz's "In Dreams Begin Responsibilities," Trilling's "The Other Margaret"; but where except in *The Dangling Man* and *The Victim* and *Augie March* do the themes and motifs of the group find full novelistic expression?

We must begin to see Bellow, then, as the inheritor of a long tradition of false starts and abject retreats and gray inconclusions. There is a sense in which he fulfills the often frustrated attempt to possess the American imagination and to enter the American cultural scene of a line of Jewish fictionists which goes back beyond the postwar generation through Ben Hecht and Ludwig Lewisohn to Abe Cahan. A hundred, a thousand one-shot novelists, ephemeral successes and baffled eccentrics stand behind him, defining a subject: the need of the Jew in America to make clear his relationship to that country in terms of belonging or protest—and a language: a speech enriched by the dialectic and joyful intellectual play of Jewish conversation.

Bellow's own story is, then, like the archetypal Jewish dream a success story since, like the standard characters in the tales of my grandfather (Socialist though he was!), the novelist, too, has "worked himself up in America." Bellow's success must not be understood, however, as exclusively his own; for he emerges at the moment when the Jews for the first time move into the center of American culture, and he must be seen in the larger context. The background is familiar enough: the gradual breaking up of the Anglo-Saxon domination of our imagination; the relentless urbanization which makes rural myths and images no longer central to our experience; the exhaustion as vital themes of the Midwest and of the movement from the provinces to New York or Chicago or Paris; the turning again from West to East, from our own heartland back to Europe; and the discovery in the Jews of a people essentially urban, essentially Europe-oriented, a ready-made image for what the American longs to or fears he is being forced to become.

On all levels in the years since World War II, the Jewish-American writer feels imposed on him the role of being The American, of registering his experience for his compatriots and for the world as The American Experience. Not only his flirtation with Communism and his disengagement, but his very sense of exclusion, his most intimate awareness of loneliness and flight are demanded of him as public symbols. The Southerner and the Jew, the homosexual out of the miasma of Mississippi and the ex-radical out of the iron landscape of Chicago and New York—these seem the exclusive alternatives, contrasting yet somehow twinned symbols of America at mid-century. *Partisan Review* becomes for Europe and *Life* magazine the mouthpiece of intellectual America, not despite but because of its tiny readership and its specially determined contributors; and in Saul Bellow a writer emerges capable of transforming its obsessions into myths.

He must not, however, be seen only in this context. His appearance as the first Jewish-American novelist to stand at the center of American literature is flanked by a host of matching successes on other levels of culture and subculture. What Saul Bellow is for highbrow literature, Salinger is for upper middlebrow, Irwin Shaw for middle middlebrow and Herman Wouk for lower middlebrow. Even on the lowbrow levels, where there has been no such truce with anti-Semitism as prosperity has brought to the middle classes, two young Jews in contriving Superman have invented for the comic books a new version of the Hero, the first purely urban incarnation of the most ancient of mythic figures. The acceptance of Bellow as the leading novelist of his generation must be paired off with the appearance of Marjorie Morningstar on the front cover of *Time*. On all levels, the Jew is in the process of being mythicized into the representative American.

There is a temptation in all this to a kind of assimilation with the most insipid values of bourgeois life in the United States. It is to

Bellow's credit that he has at once accepted the full challenge implicit in the identification of Jew with American, and yet has not succumbed to the temptation; that he has been willing to accept the burden of success without which he might have been cut off from the central subject of his time; and that he has accomplished this without essential compromise. In *Augie March,* which is the heart of his work (though technically not as successful as *The Victim* or *Seize the Day),* he has risked the final absurdity: the footloose Jewish boy, harried by urban Machiavellians, the picaresque *schlimazl* out of Fuchs or Nathanael West, becomes Huck Finn; or, if you will, Huck is transformed into the foot-loose Jewish boy. It is hard to know which way of saying it gives a fuller sense of the absurdity and importance of the transaction. The point is, I think, that the identification saves both halves of the combination from sentimental falsification: Huck Finn, who has threatened for a long time to dissolve into the snub-nosed little rascal, barefoot and overalled, and the Jewish *schlimazl,* who becomes only too easily the liberals' insufferable victim, say, Noah Ackerman in Irwin Shaw's *The Young Lions.*

The themes of Saul Bellow are not, after all, very different from those of the middlebrow Jewish novelists in step with whom he has "worked himself up"; but in treatment they become transformed. Like Wouk or Shaw, he, too, has written a War Novel: a book about the uncertainty of intellectual and Jew face to face with a commitment to regimentation and violence. But unlike Wouk and Shaw, Bellow has not merely taken the World War I novel of protest and adulterated it with popular front pieties. His intellectual is not shown up like Wouk's Keefer; his Jew does not prove himself as brave and brutal as his anti-Semitic buddies like Shaw's Ackerman or Wouk's Greenspan, whose presumable triumphs are in fact abject surrenders. The longing to relinquish the stereotyped protest of the twenties, no longer quite believed in, is present in Bellow's *Dangling Man,* but present as a *subject:* a temptation to be confronted, not a value to be celebrated.

Dangling Man is not an entirely successful book; it is a little mannered, a little incoherent, obviously a first novel. But it is fresh beyond all expectation, unlike any American war book before or since; for Bellow has realized that for his generation the war itself is an anticlimax (too foreknown from a score of older novels to be really lived), that their real experience is the waiting, the dangling, the indecision before the draft. His book therefore ends, as it should, with its protagonist about to leave for camp and writing in his journal: "Hurray for regular hours! And for the supervision of the spirit! Long live regimentation!" In the purest of ironies, the slogans of accommodation are neither accepted nor rejected, but suspended.

Similarly, in *The Victim* Bellow takes up what is, perhaps, the theme *par excellence* of the liberaloid novel of the forties: anti-Semitism. In proletarian novels, though many were written by Jews, this was a subject only peripherally treated; for the Jew in the Communist movement, Judaism was the enemy, Zionism and the Jewish religion the proper butt of satire and dissent. But Hitler had made a difference, releasing a flood of pious protests against discrimination; from Arthur Miller's *Focus* to John Hersey's *The Wall,* via *Gentleman's Agreement. The Professor's Umbrella,* etc., Jew and Gentile alike took up the subject over and over. In a time when the Worker had been replaced by the Little Man as a focus for undiscriminating sympathy, the Little Jew took his place beside the Little Negro, the Little Chinese, the Little Paraplegic as a favorite victim. Even what passed for War Novels were often merely anti-anti-Semitic fictions in disguise, the war itself being treated only as an occasion for testing a Noble Young Jew under the pressure of ignorant hostility.

In the typical middlebrow novel, it was seldom a real Jew who was exposed to persecution; rather some innocent gentile who by putting on glasses mysteriously came to look Jewish or some high-minded reporter only pretending to be a Jew. In part what is involved is the commercial necessity for finding a gimmick to redeem an otherwise overworked subject; but in part what is at stake is surely a confusion in the liberal, middlebrow mind about what a Jew is anyhow: a sneaking suspicion that Jew-baiting is real but Jews are imaginary, just as, to the same mind, witch-hunting is real but witches only fictions.

In Bellow's book about anti-Semitism, *The Victim,* once more the confusion becomes the subject. It is Asa Leventhal, not the author, who is uncertain of what it means to be a Jew because he does not know yet what it is to be a man; and neither he nor his author will be content with the simple equation: the victim equals the Jew, the Jew the victim. In *The Victim,* Jew and anti-Semite are each other's prey as they are each other's beloved. At the moment when the Jew in general, when the author himself as well as his protagonist, have moved into situations of security, however tenuous, inflicting injury in their scramble to win that security, Bellow alone among our novelists has had the imagination and the sheer nerve to portray the Jew, the Little Jew, as victimizer as well as victim. Allbee may be mad, a pathological anti-Semite and a bum, but his charge that Leventhal's success was achieved somehow at his expense is not utter nonsense. It is the necessary antidote to the self-pity of the Jew, one part of a total ambiguous picture. In the slow, gray, low-keyed exposition of *The Victim,* Leventhal's violence and his patience, his desire to exculpate himself and his sense of guilt, his haunting by the anti-Semite he haunts, become for us truths, part of our awareness of our place as Jews in the American scene.

As *The Victim* is Bellow's most specifically Jewish book, *Augie March* (in this, as in all other respects, a reaction from the former) is his most generally American. Its milieu is Jewish-American, its speech patterns somehow molded by Yiddish, but its theme is the native theme of *Huckleberry Finn:* The rejection of power and commitment and success, the pursuit of a primal innocence. It is a strangely non-Jewish book in being concerned not with a man's rise but with his evasion of rising; and yet even in that respect it reminds us of *David Levinsky,* of the criticism of David implicit in the text and entrusted to the Socialist characters. It is as if David had been granted a son, a grandson, to try again—to seek a more genuine Americanism of noncommitment. Certainly, Bellow's character is granted a symbolic series of sexual successes to balance off the sexual failures of Cahan's protagonist. But the Socialism of Cahan does not move his descendant; it has become in the meanwhile Soviet Communism, an alternative image of material success, and has failed; so that there is left to Augie only the denial of the values of capitalism without a corresponding allegiance, a desire to flee success from scene to scene, from girl to girl, from father to father—in favor of what? The most bitter of Happy Endings as well as the most negative, the truly American Happy Ending: no reunion with the family, no ultimately happy marriage, no return to the native place—only a limitless disponibility guarded like a treasure. It is, of course, the ending of *Huckleberry Finn,* an ending which must be played out as comedy to be tolerable at all; but unlike Twain, Bellow, though he has found the proper tone for his episodes, cannot recapture it for his close. *Augie,* which begins with such rightness, such conviction, does not know how to end; shriller and shriller, wilder and wilder, it finally whirls apart in a frenzy of fake euphoria and exclamatory prose.

Seize the Day is a pendant and resolution to *Augie March.* Also a study of success and failure, this time it treats them in contemporary terms rather than classic ones, reworking directly a standard middlebrow theme. Call it *The Death of a Salesman* and think of Arthur Miller. It is the price of failure in a world dedicated to success that Bellow is dealing with now; or more precisely, the self-consciousness of failure in a world where it is not only shameful but rare; or most exactly of all, the bitterness of success and failure become pawns in the deadly game between father and son. Bellow is not very successful when he attempts to deal with the sentimental and erotic relations that are the staples of the great European novels; his women tend to be nympholeptic projections, fantasies based on girls one never had; and his husbands and wives seem convincing only at the moment of parting. But he comes into his own when he turns to the emotional transactions of males inside the family: brother and brother, son and father—or father-hating son and Machiavellian surrogate father. It is the muted rage of such relationships that is the emotional stuff of his best work; and in *Seize the Day,* it is the dialogues of Tommy and his old man, Tommy and the sharper Tamkin, that move us, prepare us for Tommy's bleakest encounter: with himself and the prescience of his own death.

But how, we are left asking, has Bellow made tragedy of a theme that remains in the hands of Arthur Miller sentimentality and "good theater"? It is just this magical transformation of the most travestied of middlebrow themes which is Bellow's greatest triumph. That transformation is in part the work of style, a function of language. Bellow is in no sense an experimental writer; the scraps of *avant-garde* technique which survive in *The Dangling Man* are purged away in *The Victim;* yet he has managed to resist the impulse to lifeless lucidity which elsewhere has taken over in a literature reacting to the linguistic experiments of the twenties. There is always the sense of a living voice in his prose, for his books are all dramatic; and though this sometimes means a deliberate muting of rhetoric for the sake of characterization, it just as often provides occasions for a release of full virtuosity. Muted or released, his language is never dull or merely expedient, but always moves under tension, toward or away from a kind of rich, crazy poetry, a juxtaposition of high and low style, elegance and slang, unlike anything else in English except *Moby Dick,* though at the same time not unrelated in range and variety to spoken Yiddish.

Since Bellow's style is based on a certain conversational ideal at once intellectual and informal, dialogue is for him necessarily a distillation of his strongest effects. Sometimes one feels his characters' speeches as the main events of the books in which they occur; certainly they have the impact of words exchanged among Jews, that is to say, the impact of actions, not merely overheard but *felt,* like kisses or blows. Implicit in the direction of his style is a desire to encompass a world larger, richer, more disorderly and untrammeled than that of any other writer of his generation; it is this which impels him toward the picaresque, the sprawling, episodic manner of *Augie March.* But there is a counterimpulse in him toward the tight, rigidly organized, underplayed style of *The Victim:* and at his best, I think, as in *Seize the Day,* an ability to balance the two tendencies against each other: hysteria and catalepsy, the centrifugal and the centripetal in a sort of perilous rest.

But the triumphs of Bellow are not mere triumphs of style; sometimes indeed they must survive the collapse of that style into mannerism, mechanical self-parody. Beyond an ear, Bellow possesses a fortunate negative talent: a constitutional inability to dissolve his characters into their representative types, to compromise their individuality for the sake of a point. It is not merely that his protagonists refuse to blur into the generalized Little People, the Victims of sentimental liberalism; but that they are themselves portrayed as being conscious of their struggle against such debasement. That struggle is, indeed, the essence of their self-consciousness, their self-definition. Their invariable loneliness is felt by them and by us not only as a function of urban life and the atomization of culture, but as something *willed:* the condition and result of their search to know what they are.

More, perhaps, than any other recent novelist, Bellow is aware that the collapse of the proletarian novel, which marks the starting place of his own art, has meant more than the disappearance of a convention in the history of fiction. With the disappearance of the proletarian novel as a form there has taken place the gradual dissolution of the last widely shared definition of man: man as the product of society. If man seems at the moment extraordinarily lonely, it is not only because he finds it hard to communicate with his fellows, but because he has lost touch with any overarching definition of himself.

This Bellow realizes, as he realizes that it is precisely in such loneliness, once man learns not to endure but to *become* that loneliness, that man can rediscover his identity and his fellowship with others. We recognize the Bellow character because he is openly what we are in secret, because he is us without our customary defenses. Such a protagonist lives nowhere except in the City; he camps temporarily in boardinghouses or lonely hotels, sits by himself at the corner table of some seedy restaurant or climbs backbreaking stairways in search of another whose existence no one will admit. He is the man whose wife is off visiting her mother or has just left him; the man who returns to find his house in disorder or inhabited by a squalid derelict; the man who flees his room to follow the funeral of someone he never knew.

He is essential man, man stripped of success and belongingness, even of failure; he is man disowned by his father, unrecognized by his son, man without woman, man face to face with himself, which means for Bellow face to face not with a fact but a question: "What am I?" To which the only answer is: "He who asks!" But such a man is at once the Jew in perpetual exile and Huck Finn in whom are blended with perfect irony the twin American beliefs that the answer to all questions is always over the next horizon and that there is no answer now or ever.

—1957

The Jew in the American Novel

Foreword

THIS ESSAY is intended to be not exhaustive but representative. The few writers who are discussed at any length are those who seem to me (and my personal taste plays a role of which any reader enamored of objectivity should be warned) both most rewarding as artists and most typical as actors in the drama of Jewish cultural life in America. I have not deliberately, however, omitted as untypical any Jewish American fictionist of first excellence. I am aware of how many rather good novelists I have slighted (along with some rather bad ones whom I am glad to pass over in silence); but I will not try to list them here, thus risking further injustice to those whose names fail to come to mind.

What I hope emerges from my study is a general notion of the scope and shape of the Jewish American tradition in fiction—useful to Gentile and Jew, reader and writer alike, not merely as history but as a source of pleasure and self-knowledge. The bonus of satisfaction for the critic engaged on such a job is the privilege of saying once more how much joy and terror and truth he has found, not only in certain widely respected authors but also in such relatively neglected ones as Abraham Cahan, Daniel Fuchs and Henry Roth.

1. Zion as Eros

The novel in which the Jewish writer attempts to make meaningful fiction of his awareness of himself as a Jew in America remains for a long time of merely parochial interest. In the first fifty years of such writing, only four novelists emerge whose work seems worth remembering; yet even of these none is mentioned in the most recent standard history of the American novel. The omission does not arise from ignorance or discrimination; it is a matter of simple justice. The fiction of Sidney Luska, Abraham Cahan, Ludwig Lewisohn, and Ben Hecht appears in retrospect not merely to fall short of final excellence, but to remain somehow irrelevant to the main lines of development of fiction in the United States.

For American Jews, their achievement has, of course, a symptomatic, an historical importance since they act as surrogates for the whole Jewish-American community in its quest for an identity, a symbolic significance on the American scene. Such early novelists begin to establish an image of the Jew capable not only of satisfying the Jews themselves, but also of representing them to their Gentile neighbors. The writing of the American-Jewish novel is essentially, then, an act of assimilation: a demonstration that there is an American Jew (whose Jewishness and Americanism enrich each other) and that he feels at home!

The striving of Jews to become in the United States not merely facts of the census but also of the imagination is only half of a double process that must be seen whole to be understood at all. As the Jewish writer goes out in search of himself, he encounters the Gentile writer on a complementary quest to come to terms with the Jew, the stranger in his land. Collaborators or rivals, whether willingly or not, Jewish fictionist and Gentile engage in a common enterprise. For a long time, indeed, it is hard for the Jewish novelist to compete with the Gentile in the creation of images of Jewishness. Ludwig Lewisohn's *The Island Within* may not be recorded in the standard history, but *The Sun Also Rises* is; for it is a subtler and truer book, and Robert Cohn, middleweight boxing champion from Princeton, is a realer Jew than any of Lewisohn's. That he is the product of anti-Semitic malice rather than love is from a literary point of view irrelevant. For better or worse, it is Hemingway's image of the Jew which survives the twenties: an overgrown boy scout and hangdog lover—an outsider still, even among outsiders, and in self-imposed exile.

It is hardly surprising that as late as 1930, Gentile writers are more effective at representing American Jews than are Jews themselves; for behind them there is a longer tradition of working with the American scene, and even a longer experience in projecting images of the American Jew than we are likely to remember. The first Jewish character in American fiction is the creation of the first professional novelist in the United States, Charles Brockden Brown. In 1799, he published *Arthur Mervyn,* the protagonist of which, after two volumes of being buffeted by a stubbornly perverse destiny, finds himself with a haven in sight. Like the typical Brown hero, he is about to redeem his fortune by marriage to a woman mature and well-to-do; and like all such heroes, he addresses her more as a mother than as a bride—though this time with an overtone of terror. "As I live, my good mamma," he says gazing into the eyes of Achsa Fielding, "those eyes of yours have told me a secret. I almost think they spoke to me. . . . I might have been deceived by a fancied voice . . . but let me die if I did not think they said you were —a *Jew.*" "At this sound," the author tells us, "her features were instantly veiled with the deepest sorrow and confusion."

Arthur Mervyn has, indeed, guessed right, and for a moment the promised Happy Ending trembles in the balance; but Jewess or not, Mrs. Fielding offers too great a hope of security to be rejected, and Mervyn marries her. So sane and bourgeois a climax infuriated Shelley, who, though an admirer of Brockden Brown, could never forgive him for allowing his hero to desert an Anglo-Saxon "peasant girl" for a rich Jewish widow. Despite so prompt an appearance in American literature, however, the Jewish character does not immediately prosper, remaining an exotic or occasional figure until our own century. When present at all in classic American fiction, the image of the Jew is likely to appear, as it had in *Arthur Mervyn,* in female form—superficially just another variant of the Dark Lady, who is otherwise Mediterranean or vaguely "Oriental" (though, indeed, the term seems sometimes a mere euphemism for Jewish) or even Negro. The Ruth of Melville's long narrative poem *Clarel* or the Miriam of Hawthorne's *The Marble Faun* are, like Brockden Brown's prototype, dark projections of sexual experience or allure, foils to the pale, Anglo-Saxon maiden. Though objects of great erotic potency, they do not ordinarily survive to their book's endings, being death-ridden as well as death-bearing, but are consigned to imprisonment or an early grave.

The American writer is attracted toward the archetypal pattern of Shylock and Jessica, the sinister Jew deprived of his lovely daughter; but he cannot treat it with the comic aplomb of Shakespeare or even the Romantic blitheness of Scott. In his work, a tragic blight falls over the Gentile myth of assimilation, the dream of rescuing the desirable elements in the Judaic tradition (maternal tenderness and exotic charm: the figure of Mary) from the unsympathetic (patriarchal rigor and harsh legalism: the figure of the High Priest and Father Abraham). Indeed, except as the threatening guardians of sloe-eyed ambiguous beauties, male Jewish characters seldom make more than peripheral appearances in earlier American fiction. There are neither American Riahs nor Fagins though one of the villains in George Lippard's *The Quaker City, or the Monks of Monk Hall* is called, unsubtly enough, Gabriel von Gelt. ("Vot you scratch your fingersh on te floor? Hey?" Gabriel is reported as saying in the earliest of literary "Jewish accents.")

This novel, an astonishing blend of home-grown socialism, violence, and genteel pornography, appeared in 1844 and won rapidly an immense number of readers, who probably did not single out the lone Jew from the crew of thugs who run a Gothic whorehouse for the off-hours amusement of Philadelphia's respectable citizens. Yet it is not unimportant that in the nightmare phantasmagoria of the populist imagination run wild—among the hunchback dwarfs, deaf and dumb Negroes, corrupt clergymen, and millionaires gloating over the bared breasts of drugged virgins—the figure of the hawk-nosed, conniving Jew takes his due place. Gabriel von Gelt is the ancestor of the fictional Jewish gangster, the Wolfsheim, say, of Fitzgerald's *The Great Gatsby*.

Long before the Jewish novelist existed in America, at any rate, the Jewish character had been invented, and had frozen into the anti-Jewish stereotype. Indeed, one of the problems of the practicing Jewish-American novelist arises from his need to create his protagonists not only out of the life he knows, but *against* the literature on which he, and his readers, have been nurtured. In order to become a novelist, the American Jew must learn a language (learn it not as his teachers teach it, but as he speaks it with his own stubborn tongue) more complex than a mere lexicon of American words. He must assimilate a traditional vocabulary of images and symbols, changing even as he approaches it—must use it, against the grain as it were, tó create a compelling counter-image of the Jew, still somehow authentically American.

No wonder Jews are not only businessmen and workers, trade-union officials and lawyers, psychoanalysts and theater-owners but even actors, singers, musicians, composers of popular songs and makers of movies before they are writers. First the world of work and commerce, then of the professions, next that of popular culture, and only last of all, that of serious literature opens up to the American Jew. He can make the nation's songs like Irving Berlin or define its dream of the vamp like Theda Bara; he can even provide the *ersatz* of fiction like Fannie Hurst or Edna Ferber, act out for the laughs travesties of himself on the vaudeville stage with Smith and Dale or in the *Saturday Evening Post* with Montague Glass's Potash and Perlmutter. On such a level he speaks neither as a Jew becoming an American nor as an American who was a Jew; he communicates in the nonlanguage of anticulture, becomes his own stereotype. It is for this reason that the popular arts in the United States continue to this day to speak with a stage "Jewish accent." This is, however, only one more hindrance in the way of the serious Jewish writer, who must come to terms not only with Achsa Fielding and Gabriel von Gelt, but also with Sophie Tucker and Eddie Cantor.

Yet even before the triumph of the Jews in the world of mass culture, even before the perfection of the movies which sealed that victory, the Jewish-American novel had been created, the Jewish-American writer invented. The author of this achievement was, however, a *goy*—one of the most elusive and riddling figures in all American literature. He emerges in the 1880's out of those rather high-minded, assimilationist circles in German-Jewish New York, in which Ethical Culture seemed to promise a revivifying intellectual movement, at once secular and morally committed, Jewish and American. The name on the title pages of his "Jewish" books *(As It Was Written, Mrs. Peixada, The Yoke of the Thorah,* etc.) is Sidney Luska, a pseudonym obviously intended to suggest that the writer was himself Jewish; but he had apparently been born Henry Harland, a Protestant American, as discontented with his past, as uncertain of his identity as any alienated Jew. There is a certain appropriate irony in the fact that the first Jewish-American novelist was not a Jew at all, or that, more precisely, he was the creation of his own fiction, an imaginary Jew.

It is not easy to find the truth about so elusive an existence. Henry Harland was above all else an inveterate poseur, a liar who lied for his soul's sake; and the ordinary biographical sources are likely to contain whatever fabrication suited his view of himself at the moment he was asked for information. The ordinarily quite dependable *Dictionary of National Biography,* for instance, reports that Harland was born in St. Petersburg, that he was educated in Rome and studied at the University of Paris, "acquiring a knowledge of the life of the Latin Quarter"; the groundless romance of a provincial aesthete. Actually, he seems to have been born in Connecticut, to have moved early in life to New York, to have attended the Harvard Divinity School for one year—and then to have fallen under the influence of Felix Adler, who changed his whole life.

There still exists in my own mind a vestigial doubt (unsupported by any fact I have been able to discover) that Luska-Harland may, after all, have been a Jew pretending to be a Gentile pretending to be a Jew; it would be the best joke of all! More probably, however, he was a refugee from Protestantism who passed via Ethical Culture into the German-Jewish society of late nineteenth-century New York, and who tried even growing what he liked to think of as a "Jewish beard" to pass for a Jew. His books are Jewish not only in theme and point of view, but are meticulously documented with references to Jewish-American customs and to the rituals of Judaism. In one of his novels, the pursuit of verisimilitude (or exoticism!) is carried to the point of printing the name of God only as the two letter abbreviation used in Hebrew to avoid profaning the Holy Name.

Though he is now almost forgotten, Luska was in his own day a success, hailed not only by self-conscious spokesmen for Jewish culture, but greeted by William Dean Howells himself as one of the most promising younger realists. At the peak of his first fame, however, Luska committed a kind of suicide, becoming once again Henry Harland and fleeing America in one of the earliest acts of literary expatriation. He reappeared in England as the editor of *The Yellow Book,* chief journal of the *fin de siècle,* in which his own crepuscular prose (a new collection of his work was called *Grey Roses)* appeared beside the elegantly obscene decorations of Aubrey Beardsley. Harland proved to be a first-rate editor, printing, among other representatives of the advanced literature of his time, Henry James, who responded with a grateful tribute to Harland's own fiction; but his old schizoid doubts about who he was were not allayed by his new role.

During his entire term on the magazine, he wrote letters to himself signed "The Yellow Dwarf," attacking his own editorial policy. Only he knew the identity of this constant critic and relished, as he had before, his own secret duplicity. Still restless, however, he felt impelled to move once more, this time quite out of anglosaxondom, to France, where he was converted to Catholicism and ended by writing a best-seller called *The Cardinal's Snuffbox.* This piece of pseudo-aristocratic, pious fluff, whose title reveals its appeal for the provincials Harland had left behind, earned him $75,000 in its first year and enabled him to live out his life in elegant conversation amid the elegant bricabrac of pre-World War I Europe.

In his final reincarnation, he was asked once by a reporter about Sidney Luska and answered, "I never knew a Sidney Luska . . . ," and spoke of a nightmare, dimly remembered, from which he was now awakened. There is, indeed, something sufficiently nightmarish about the whole episode, though it is from this nightmare that the Jewish novel in the United States begins. But what precisely did Henry Harland dream himself in that bad dream from which it took him so long to wake? He dreamed himself the excluded artist, poor, passionate, gifted and antibourgeois, offering to a world that rebuffed him the dowry of sensibility and insight amassed by an ancient suffering race. For Harland, such mythic Jews seemed to promise the redemption of American culture, a revitalization of American life. But where were they to be found outside of his own books?

He thought, perhaps, that he had discovered the embodiment of his ideal in Felix Adler and in his own deepest self which Adler had revealed to him; but actually Harland's Jewish heroes seem to have been derived first of all from literature. The protagonist of his first book, *As It Was Written: A Jewish Musician's Story,* seems to have been suggested by the Daniel Deronda of George Eliot, who was one of Harland's favorite writers. But that oddly sexless portrait of the female artist as a Young Jew he naturalized to the American scene endowed him with a particularly American mission. "It is the Jewish element that will leaven the whole lump . . ." he writes in his novel. "The English element alone is, so to speak, one portion of pure water; the German element one portion of *eau sucrée;* now add the Jewish—it is a dose of rich strong wine. . . . The future Americans, thanks to the Jew in them, will have passions, enthusiasms. They will paint great pictures, compose great music, write great poems, be capable of great heroism. . . ." In such praise lurks an implicit threat. What if the Jew refuses the obligation, rejects even the assimilation which is the first step demanded of him in his role of secular savior?

Harland-Luska does not at first face up to this question; but there is present in his work from the start an undertone of hostility, lurking beneath the exaggerated philo-Semitism of the surface. Though his conscious mind writes the editorials that make the avowed point of his fictions, his ambivalent unconscious is writing the plots. Ernest Neuman, the artist of *A Jewish Musician's Story,* is only one-half artist; the other half is murderer! He is a Jekyll and Hyde character not merely because the exigencies of Harland's Gothic plot demand it, but because the deeper exigencies of Harland's divided mind demanded that plot to begin with. Neuman is a schizophrenic who has murdered his wife and remains unaware of it, who is consciously horrified and baffled until an experiment in automatic writing reveals to him, and to us, his guilt. This "new man," the new Jewish-American proposed as a symbol of assimilation, of the mating of the Jewish and American psyche, ends by killing his Gentile bride and proves capable only of destruction.

In *Mrs. Peixada,* Harland does permit the mating of Gentile and Jew, though he returns to the pattern of Brockden Brown and makes his symbol of Judaism a woman. It is always easier to breach the barriers against intermarriage in the popular mind by permitting the assimilation of the forbidden group through the female rather than through the male. So in the the earliest novel, marriages of aristocrats and lower-class women were applauded, while the Lady who ran off with her groom was held up as an object of contempt; and so now in the movies, Marlon Brando is allowed a Japanese wife, but his abandoned Caucasian girl is forbidden anything more than sympathetic conversation with a Japanese male. At any rate, Mrs. Peixada represents the return of the Jessica-figure in her American form; though this time she is not only stained by sexual experience (she is a widow, of course, rather than anything less genteel), she is the murderer of her first husband. Legally, to be sure, she is innocent, having acted in self-defense against that husband, who is the monstrous projection of all the evil ever attributed by the Gentile mind to the Jew: a pawnbroker, "gaunt as a skeleton . . . a hawk's beak for a nose, a hawk's beak inverted for a chin—lips, two thin, blue, crooked lines across his face, with yellow fangs behind them. . . ."

But there is worse to come. Though Luska was able to maintain in his mind not only Shylock and Jessica, but Daniel Deronda as well—nightmare and idealization in a dreamlike truce—none of those mythic figures could survive the intrusion of real Jews. Real Jews do, however, take over in *The Yoke of the Thorah*, which is perhaps the first genuine genre study of American-Jewish life in the New World. They are no longer mere projections of Anglo-Saxon self-hatred or guilt, these German-Jewish merchants of the eighties, eating, matchmaking, talking over the market. They are coarse, vulgar, platitudinous, loud, sentimental, gregarious, not saviors at all but only human beings; and the character who represents Harland moving among them shrivels and withdraws in their presence. But he cannot help listening to them, and catches for the first time (ironically, *loses* by catching) what is to be the real material of the Jewish writer.

> "Oh my daughter," Mrs. Morgenthau returned. "She works like a horse. . . . And such a *good* girl. Only nineteen years old and earns more than a hundred dollars a month. . . . She's grand. She's an angel."
>
> "Tillie's all wool from head to foot," put in Mr. Koch, "and a yard wide."

"Such a brilliant musician," said Elias.

"Musician," echoed her mother. "Well, I should say so. You ought to hear her play when she really knuckles down to it. Why you—you'd jump, you'd get so excited. The other night she was only drumming—for fun. I tell you what you do. You come around and call on us some evening."

Where now is the "rich strong wine"? Even music, which represented for Harland the essence of Jewish genius, becomes in such scenes bait in the matrimonial trap and matrimony itself merely an adjunct of business. Such an insight into the discrepancy between the traditional mission of the Jew and his actual accommodation to the American scene might have provided Harland the cue for genuine comedy or tragedy; it became instead merely the occasion for personal disillusion. It is hard to tell whether he is more distressed because the Jews will not assimilate to his heroic, artistic ideal or because they have already assimilated to the actual values of the world around them. Their very vitality parodies the American mores they accept; and face to face with that vitality as it exists not in the imaginary artist but in the real businessman, Harland experiences only a desire to go away.

The divorce to which this desire will eventually lead him is already signalled in *The Yoke of the Thorah*. The fable is a simple one: a young Jew, talented but weak and superstitious, is bullied out of marrying a sensitive and beautiful Gentile girl by the chicanery of his uncle who is a rabbi. He marries instead the gross daughter of a family of German-Jewish merchants; and having rejected a union with the Gentile world which would have redeemed him, dies lonely and disenchanted. His final gesture is to commit suicide in the middle of Central Park; but that gesture only acknowledges the fact that inwardly he had died long since. The publication of such a book by their former champion and literary hope apparently stirred the Jews of New York to bitterness. They had taken Harland in, and he had turned on them and attacked them —quite as their own writers would do in the years to come. That his attack was rooted in a burgeoning anti-Semitism, Harland himself did not at first realize; but he arose to defend himself in public forums at Jewish synagogues and temples and even wrote a couple of other "Jewish" books, quite innocent of innuendo or offense.

He was, however, really through; he had exhausted Jewishness as a subject and as a mask and was preparing for his next removal. In England and in France, he exiles the Jews from the center of his fiction to its periphery, and his last word on the subject is a casual sneer in the book that made his fortune. The words are put into the mouth of a lovely though improbable lady with an equally improbable Italian title, his gentle heroine: "The estate fell into the hands of the Jews, as everything more or less does sooner or later; and if you can believe me—they were going to turn the castle into . . . one of those monstrous, modern hotels, for other Jews to come to." The sentence foreshadows one theme of a somewhat later and certainly much greater expatriate American, with similar yearnings for orthodoxy and "the tradition."

> And the Jew squats on the window sill, the owner,
> Spawned in some estaminet of Antwerp.

> . . . On the rialto once
>   The rats are underneath the piles. The Jew is underneath the lot.

The history of Henry Harland is, finally, even more ridiculous than pathetic, a success story in the end: From Rags to Riches, from Ethical Culture on the East Side to Roman Catholicism on the Riviera. Yet before his last metamorphosis, Harland had defined what was to be the obsessive theme of the American-Jewish novel through the twenties: the theme of intermarriage, with its ambiguous blending of the hope of assimilation and the threat of miscegenation. The tradition that begins with Luska-Harland descends in one line to *The Island Within* and in another to the Cohens and the Kellys and *Abie's Irish Rose*.

It is self-evident that the Jewish-American novel in its beginnings must be a problem novel, and its essential problems must be those of identity and assimilation. The very concept of such a novel involves an attempt to blend two traditions, to contribute to the eventual grafting of whatever still lives in Judaism onto an ever-developing Americanism. One cannot, however, propose to lose himself without raising the question of what the self is which may be surrendered or kept; and the Jewish-American writer who is, of course, almost necessarily non-orthodox finds a riddle in the place where he looks for an answer. *Is* there a Jewish identity which survives the abandonment of ghetto life and ghetto beliefs, which for so long defined the Jew? Or has the Jew left in Europe, along with the pain and squalor he fled, the possibility of any definition?

What is unexpected is that these problems be posed in terms of sexual symbols, that the Jewish-American novel before 1930 be erotic fiction. The approach to and retreat from the Gentile community, the proffering of himself and the shying away out of fear of acceptance or rejection, becomes in the imagination of the Jewish writer a kind of wooing, an act of timid and virginal love. It becomes associated in his thinking with his attitude toward the new sexual freedom offered him by the breakdown of ghetto life and with the erotic subject matter that takes a central place in art once religion has been replaced as the essential subject. The Jewish-American novelist begins his attempts at a moment when the triumphs of European naturalism make it possible for fiction in the United States to break through the taboos of gentility, when the antibourgeois writer, in particular, delights in portraying himself as the exponent of the instinctual life, as the lover.

There is a real pathos in the efforts of the Jewish intellectual to see himself as Don Juan, an essential vanity in his striving to embody current theories of sexual freedom. There is nothing, either in his own deepest traditions or in the stereotypes imposed on him by Western fiction, to justify such a mythicization of himself: Shylock as Don Juan, Rashi as Don Juan, Daniel Deronda as Don Juan—they are all equally improbable. Yet it is in the role of passionate lover that the American-Jewish novelist sees himself at the moment of his entry into American literature; and the community with which he seeks to unite himself he sees as the *shikse.* Don Juan and the *shikse*—it is this legend, this improbable recasting of Samson and Delilah, which underlies American-Jewish fiction up to the end of the twenties.

The erotic theme had already been proposed by Henry Harland, and it is taken up again by Abraham Cahan in *The Rise of David Levinsky,* certainly the most distinguished novel written by an American Jew before the 1930's. It is easy to forget the sense in which Cahan's book is a love story, or even more precisely a story of the failure of love; for superficially it is another up-from-the-ghetto book, its concerns chiefly social. Indeed, it appeared in 1917, the year of the Russian Revolution, when for a little while it seemed possible that the dream of Socialism might become a fact and the Jew really assimilate to the emancipated Human Race instead of to the nation in which he happened to find himself. No wonder that even the more perspicuous critics were content to talk about *David Levinsky* as a social document: a commentary on the rise of the garment industry and its impact on American life; a study of the crisis in American-Jewish society when the first wave of German immigrants were being overwhelmed by Jews from Galicia and the Russian Pale; a case history of the expense of spirit involved in changing languages and cultures; a portrayal of New World secularism which made of City College a Third Temple and of Zionism and Marxism enlightened religions for those hungry for an orthodoxy without God.

Certainly, *David Levinsky* is all these things, as it is also the account of a Jew who dissipated the promise of his life in the pursuit of wealth; it is a rich and complex book, a retrospective and loving essay on the failures of his people by a man nearly sixty when he wrote it. An anti-Semitic book, the conservative Jewish reviewers blindly called it: "Had the book been published anonymously, we might have taken it for cruel caricature of a hated race by some anti-Semite. . . ." It is to remain the typical response of the "guardians of the Jewish Community" to any work which treats with art and candor the facts of Jewish life in the United States. Both the traditions of the European naturalist novel, on which Cahan really drew, and those of the American novel, to which he aspired, prescribe for the author a "negative" attitude toward the philistine society around him; and as a Jew he found especially abhorrent the drift of his own people, the chosen remnant, toward delusive bourgeois values. The disenchantment that became anti-Semitism in the imaginary Jew, Harland, becomes in Cahan a prophetic rage which is really love, an apparent treason which is the profoundest loyalty. In this respect, he remains the model for all serious Jewish-American novelists.

His ultimate subject is, aptly enough, loneliness: the loneliness of the emancipated Jew, who has lost the shared alienation of the ghetto to become a self-declared citizen of a world which rejects even as it rewards him. The unique loneliness of the "successful" immigrant Jew, however, suggests to Cahan the common human loneliness of those who have failed at love; and in the end it is hard to tell with which loneliness his book is primarily concerned. It is with the melancholy of David Levinsky that the novel begins; he came to America, he tells us, with four cents in his pocket and has now $2,000,000, but his life is "devoid of significance." To explain his joylessness David has certain theories. It is all due, he insists, to "a streak of sadness in the blood of my race"; to be a Jew is to be sad! But he asserts, too, that it is his wealth and the devices by which he has pursued it that have cut him off from the sources of happiness: "There are cases when success is a tragedy."

Yet Cahan makes the point with some care that David is only *incidentally* a capitalist, that he is not fundamentally different from other immigrant Jews of his generation who have become trade-unionists and socialists; what is peculiar in his development has occurred almost by accident. "Had I chanced to hear a socialist speech," he says at one point, "I might have become an ardent follower of Karl Marx." Instead he read Spencer and Darwin! What, then, is *essentially* wrong with David? Cahan does not answer unequivocally, but at times at least he suggests that he is somehow sexually or affectively incapacitated; that no boy brought up in the Talmudic tradition "that to look at the finger of a woman in desire is equivalent to seeing her whole body naked" can enter into the full heritage of modernity, which includes an ideal of sexual freedom as well as the hope of a classless society. Like Peretz, he considers the vestiges of ghetto Puritanism one of the hindrances that stand between the Jew and his full humanity.

Each failure of David Levinsky at winning a woman (and the book is in effect a tally of such failures) is given a symbolic social meaning. He does not get Matilda, his first love whom he desires while still in Europe, because he is not yet sufficiently emancipated from his Talmudic training; he cannot keep Dora, the wife of a friend with whom he carries on an inconclusive affair, because he has stepped outside of the Jewish family and cannot smuggle his way back in; he cannot win Anna Tevkin, young socialist and daughter of an eminent Hebrew poet, because he has learned to sing *The Star-Spangled Banner* with tears in his eyes, because he is a "Good American."

But for all his "Americanism," he remains still in some baffling sense a Jew and is, therefore, forbidden the possibility of marrying a Gentile. His last real chance at love seems, indeed, to be offered him by a Gentile woman "of high character," who all but proposes to him; yet at the last moment he feels between them "a chasm of race." There is always something! Though he cannot abide loneliness and prowls the streets ("I dream of marrying some day. I dread to think of dying a lonely man. Sometimes I have a spell of morbid amativeness and seem to be falling in love with woman after woman. . . ."), it is no use; some deep impotence dogs him. They are not symbols only, these failed love affairs of David Levinsky; they are real failures of the flesh and spirit, failures of a Jew in love with love and money.

In Ludwig Lewisohn and Ben Hecht, the two most admired Jewish novelists of the twenties, the erotic theme is restated in exaggerated, almost hysterical tones. There is something about their work not merely brash and provocative (this they intended), but vulgar and crude; and it becomes hard to remember that they seemed once the most promising of young novelists, before one was translated into a prophet of the new Zion and the other into a maker of successful movies. "More gross talent than net accomplishment," a disgruntled critic finally said of Hecht, and the phrase will do for Lewisohn, too. They chose to begin with such different masks, the professor and the reporter, that it is difficult to see how much they had in common, how both contrived sexual melodramas to project the plight of the Jew in the Jazz Age. A pair of titles, however, Lewisohn's *Don Juan* (1923) and Hecht's *A Jew in Love* (1931), frame the period and define its chief concern.

Unlike Cahan, who preceded them, and the Proletarian novelists, who were to follow them, Lewisohn and Hecht are hostile to Marxism; and the Marxists (most of them Jewish, of course) who appear in their books are portrayed as self-deceivers, attempting to conceal their personal anguish behind an artificial fog of socialist cant. The secular Jewish prophet honored by Hecht and Lewisohn is not Marx but Freud; and the secular religion to which they respond is what they call Freudianism, though, like many intellectuals in their time, they were not quite sure where Freud ends and D. H. Lawrence begins. Psychoanalysis seemed to them primarily one more device for mocking the middle class, one more source for arguments in defense of sexual emancipation. Beyond this, their interest remained superficial. Lewisohn's novel, *The Island Within,* contains what is probably the most unconvincing psychoanalyst in literature and manages to tuck away an utterly improbable description of an analysis, somewhere between its "epical" beginning and the little sermon on mixed marriages with which it ends.

Their common devotion to Eros and to Freud as his prophet, Lewisohn and Hecht develop in quite different ways. Lewisohn sets his in a context of belated German Romanticism, from which he derives a mystique of passion somehow synthesized with internationalism, pacifism, and a Crocean commitment to art. Hecht, on the other hand, adjusts his to a provincial version of *symbolisme,* which means for him a dedication to disorder and cynicism in art and life. Celebrated in his day as a new American Huysmans, he has become for us undistinguishable from the pressroom heroes of his *Front Page,* flip hard-guys to whom whiskey is the Muse and Chicago the Earthly Paradise. Lewisohn typically identifies himself with his protagonists, harried by women and bourgeois taboos, but pledged to fight for freedom with the sole weapon of art; Hecht presumably separates himself from the scoundrels who are the heroes of his books, though he covertly sympathizes with their amoral contempt for decency and tenderness.

The leading characters of both, though presumably intellectuals, are notable not for their ideas but for their efforts, successful or baffled, to find in themselves the demonic, impulsive sources of life. In this they are the authentic products of their age, though uneasy projections of their Jewish authors. What has a Jew to do finally with the primitivism and phallic mysticism which possessed the era? Only when he revolts not merely against philistinism but against his own most authentic traditions can he espouse such a cause. It is illuminating to remember that writers like D. H. Lawrence and Sherwood Anderson, the real high priests of the erotic religion, portrayed Jews in their fiction as natural enemies of the primitive ideal, antitypes of the passionate hero: cold, cerebral, incapable of the dark surrender of the self.

It is true enough that when Lewisohn uses *Don Juan* as a book title, he does so ironically and that he somehow feels obliged to pretend (however unconvincingly) that his protagonist is not a Jew; but he is all the while *living* the role in his own much-publicized life. In the news and gossip columns as well as in the pages of his novels, Lewisohn concentrated on justifying his love life—with time off for belaboring the poor women who failed him and the divorce laws which hampered his style. The only subject to which Lewisohn responds in his fiction with real fervor, the single spring of his creative work, is his own sex life desperately projected as typical.

The Island Within, his attempt at a major novel, opens with a manifesto declaring his epic ambitions and defending them against the proponents of the novel of sensibility, just then replacing the older, objective form. His declared intent is esthetically reactionary enough, but he cannot abide even by that; before the book is half over, he has abandoned the broad-canvas portrayal of three generations of Jewish life in Poland and Germany for a more intimate evocation of modern marital difficulties, for his usual blend of self-pity and editorial. No sooner has he reached America, than he heads for the bedroom, the old battle ground on which the sensitive Jew, a psychoanalyst this time, still struggles with the *shikse* (in the teeth of public opinion and benighted law) for the possession of his own soul.

Hecht, on the other hand, goes immediately to his theme—in this case not a direct exculpation of himself but the satirizing of another, a successful Jew. When the book first appeared, it was read as a *roman à clef;* and those in the know were more than willing to let the ignorant in on the secret of who Jo Bosshere, the publisher-protagonist, *really* was. At this point, when we no longer care about such revelations, it becomes clear that the book is more than a wicked jibe at an identifiable public figure; it is a work of inspired self-hatred: a portrait of the Jewish author as his own worst (Jewish) enemy. At any rate, the hero of Hecht's novel, whose original name was Abe Nussbaum, juggles a wife, a mistress, a whore whom he really loves, the wife of a good friend, in a frenzy of erotic machiavellianism, behind which there is no real desire. He braces himself for each sexual encounter with an energy so neurotically tense that it is dissipated by a knock at the door, a chance remark, the slightest shift in affective tone. What drives him is not passion but the need to force from the world unwilling avowals of love for his absurdly horrifying Jewish face. Bosshere-Nussbaum is portrayed by Hecht as the caricature of the anti-Semite come to life: not merely the Jew, but the nightmare of the Jew (as hawkbeaked and vulpine as Mr. Peixada) as Don Juan.

Of all the women he has possessed without desire, the one to whom Bosshere most desperately clings is, of course, the single *shikse* among them: the pure blonde tantalizing image of a world which all of his assaults and betrayals cannot make his own. Toward her he is impelled by something deeper than sadism and self-hatred, by what Hecht calls brutally "the niggerish delight of the Jew in the blonde." If he is defeated in the end, however, it is not because of the resistance of his *shikse* so much as because of his own inability to accept himself as the seducer and scoundrel. "To himself he was only this greedy, monogamous Jew full of biblical virtues. . . ." To himself he was only the child of his people, not a great lover but a martyr to women, who cries out finally in the unexpected scriptural allusion, "My God, my God, why hast Thou forsaken me," and does not know whether he is invoking Eros or the God of Abraham, Isaac, and Jacob.

This is implicitly at least a self-criticism of the Jewish intellectual that cuts much deeper than personal satire, but it is marred by an imprecision of language and an uncertainty of tone that ends in incoherence. Lewisohn is explicit, however pat and superficial, and in *The Island Within* (actually published three years before *A Jew in Love)* he gives to the erotic-assimilationist novel its final form. Arthur Levy, the protagonist of Lewisohn's novel, never abandons his vocation as a lover; he merely transfers his desire from the representative of an alien world to the symbol of his own people, thus reinforcing a battered Romantic faith in sexual passion with an equally Romantic commitment to Zionism. As he has earlier combined the advocacy of sexual freedom with a vaguely internation-alist humanism, so now he combines it with a revived Judaism, adapted to the modern scientific mind.

He pretends, indeed, to find in the Jewish tradition sanctions for his view of love. Is not Jewish divorce, he asks rhetorically, eas-ier than Christian? Were not the Jews always skeptical about the notion of marriage as a sacrament? Have Jewish women historically not represented a *tertium quid:* neither servile like the slave-women of the Anglo-Saxon world before modern times, nor hope-lessly lost like the "emancipated" Gentile women of the current era? Have they not remained at the heart of the tradition the Jewish intellectual has temporarily abandoned, waiting to bestow on him when he returns the warm fulfillment he has vainly sought in strangers? We have come full circle from Cahan's view of ghetto Judaism as a castrating force.

But Lewisohn is prepared to go even further than this, from a defense of Zion as the true Eros, to an attack on the Gentile woman as the false Aphrodite. It has all been the fault of the *shikse* and of the Jewish intellectual only so far as he has become her victim. It is no longer the Gentile world which rejects the Jew in Lewisohn's fic-tion (that world is, indeed, eager to draw him in and suck him dry), but the Jew who rejects it—even as Arthur Levy rejects the hope of assimilation and sets out at his story's end back to Europe, back to his people's past, to investigate the plight of his fellow Jews in Rumania.

We have reached at last the reverse of Harland-Luska's theory in *The Yoke of the Thorah;* Jessica has yielded to Delilah. Not by rejecting the Gentile girl for the Jewish one but by preferring her, the sensitive Jew commits spiritual suicide. The *shikse* represents no longer the promise of fulfillment, of a blending of cultures, but only the threat of death, of the loss of identity. The reversal, how-ever, like the original thesis, remains a little too pat, more suited for sermonizing than poetry; at any rate, in neither case did the authors make of their themes moving and memorable fictions. Yet with Lewisohn's establishment of the antistereotype in its classic form something has been accomplished, that is to say, the last possibility of the erotic-assimilationist novel has been exhausted. His novel rests like a melancholy capstone on the whole period which reaches from the eighties to the dying twenties, a monument to an unsuccessful quest by whose example later writers have profited. After *The Island Within,* the Jewish-American novelist knew at least one direction in which he could not go.

2. Zion as Armageddon

Though there were American Jewish novelists of real distinction in the first three decades of the twentieth century, it is not until the thirties that such writers play a critical role in the total development of American literature. From that point on, they have felt themselves and have been felt by the general public as more than pioneers and interlopers, more than exotics and eccentrics. Indeed, the patterns of Jewish speech, the experiences of Jewish childhood and adolescence, the smells and tastes of the Jewish kitchen, the sounds of the Jewish synagogue have become, since 1930, staples of the American novel.

It is, of course, Jewish urban life in particular which has provided a standard décor for the novel: the life of New York, and especially of the ghettos of the East Side, Williamsburg, etc. In a certain sense, indeed, the movement of Jewish material from the periphery to the center is merely one phase of a much larger shift within the world of the American novel: that urbanization of our fiction which accompanies the urbanization of our general culture.

Our literary twenties were dominated by provincial writers like Theodore Dreiser, Sherwood Anderson, and Sinclair Lewis, even Faulkner and Hemingway, who close that period and provide a bridge into the age that succeeds it. Whatever their talent, they remained essentially country boys who had come to the big city, who had wandered under their own power into New Orleans or New York, who had been transported by the A.E.F. to Paris. Whether they stayed or returned home again did not finally matter; even when they wrote about the city, they wrote about it as seen through the eyes of one who had come late into it and had remained a stranger.

Despite an occasional sport like Myron Brinig, who writes about Montana, or MacKinlay Kantor, whose subject matter includes hound dogs, Jewish writers do not fit into such a provincial pattern, which does not, in any case, reflect the typical, the *mythical* Jewish experience in America. Their major entry into the American novel had to await its urbanization, though that entry is not, to be sure, only a function of such urbanization. It is an extension, too, of the break-up of the long-term Anglo-Saxon domination of our literature which began in the generation just before the First World War. The signal that this double process had started was the emergence of Dreiser as the first novelist of immigrant stock to take a major position in American fiction. There is something ironic in the fact that the breach through which succeeding Jewish writers poured was opened by one not innocent of anti-Semitism; but once the way was opened for immigrants in general, it was possible for Jews to follow.

At any rate, by the end of the thirties (a recent historian of Jewish literature points out) there were some sixty American Jewish writers of fiction who could be called without shameless exaggeration "prominent." A close examination of that historian's list proves rather disheartening; for of the sixty-odd names he mentions, fewer than ten seem to me worthy of remembering; and three of these (Abe Cahan, Ludwig Lewisohn and Ben Hecht) belong, in theme and significance, to the twenties in which their major work was accomplished. The writers who remain of the original sixty are Edward Dahlberg, Leonard Ehrlich, Daniel Fuchs, Meyer Levin (recently come to life by reaching back into the Jewish Society of the twenties for an image of violence and disgust stark enough to move us) and Henry Roth. Even if one were to add to these certain others not included in the original group, say, Waldo Frank, Maurice Samuel, Isidor Schneider and Michael Gold, who are at least symptomatically important, it would make a constellation by no means inspiring; for no one of them is a figure of first importance even in the period itself.

Fuchs and Roth are writers of considerable talent, even of major talent, perhaps; but for various reasons, their achievement is limited. Roth is the author of a single novel, *Call It Sleep;* and

Fuchs, though he wrote three before his retreat to Hollywood and popular fiction for ladies' magazines (and despite a recent comeback in short fiction) wrote only one book of considerable scope: *Homage to Blenholt*. There remains, of course, Nathan Wallenstein Weinstein, who preferred to call himself Nathanael West—and whose long neglect by official writers on the period is now being overbalanced by his enthusiastic rediscoverers. For a long time, scarcely anyone but Henry Popkin* considered him worth touting; but now the republication of his whole works and his translation into a Broadway play have given West back a full-scale existence. There is no use being carried away, however, no use in concealing from ourselves the fact that what has been restored to us is only another tragically incomplete figure, whose slow approach to maturity ends in death. And there remains further the troublesome question: is West in any effective sense a Jew?

Though the thirties mark the mass entry of the Jewish writer into American fiction, they do not last long enough to see any major triumphs. There is no Jewish writer among the recognized reigning figures of the period: no Dos Passos, no Farrell, no Steinbeck; there is no Jewish writer who played a comparable role to the continuing major novelists of the twenties: no Fitzgerald, no Hemingway, no Faulkner. There is no Jewish author (with the possible exception of West) who can rank even with middle-generation fictionists like Robert Penn Warren, who seemed at the end of the thirties promising young men.

Even in the creation of images of the Jew, a job the Jewish writer in the United States has long been struggling to take out of the hands of the Gentiles, there is no Jewish writer who can compare in effectiveness to Thomas Wolfe. Just as Sherwood Anderson and Hemingway and Fitzgerald succeeded in making their hostile images of Jews imaginative currencies in the twenties, Wolfe succeeded in imposing on his period a series of portraits derived from his experiences at New York University: enameled Jewesses with melon breasts; crude young male students pushing him off the side-

---

* I have in conversation, as well as through reading his articles, so long exchanged ideas with Henry Popkin on the American Jewish novelist that I am indebted to him everywhere.

walk; hawkbeaked Jewish elders, presumably manipulating the world of wealth and power from behind the scenes.

What, then, was the modest contribution of the Jewish writer to the fiction of the thirties, and how did this prepare for later successes going beyond anything he himself achieved? Predictably enough, a large number of American Jewish writers of the period were engaged in the production of the best-advertised (though, alas, quite infertile) art-product of the period: the Proletarian Novel. Perhaps the best way to define that subform of the novel is to remind ourselves that it is the major result of applying to the creation of literature the theory that "art is a weapon"; and that therefore it was in intent anti-art, or at least, opposed to everything which "petty-bourgeois formalism" considered art to be. Perhaps because of the contradictions inherent in such a view, it had one of the shortest lives ever lived by a literary genre. One speaks of the Proletarian Novel as a form of the thirties, but in fact it was finished by 1935 or 1936, becoming at that point merely formula writing, completely at the mercy of political shifts inside the Communist movement.

In any case, the Proletarian Novel is not, as its name suggests, merely a book about proletarians; it is alternatively about poor farmers, members of the lower middle class; and most often, in *fact* if not in theory, about intellectuals, specifically about the intellectual's attempt to identify himself with the oppressed and with the Movement which claimed to represent them. The Proletarian Novel was, then, ideological fiction dedicated to glorifying the Soviet Union and the Communist Party and to proving that the Party was the consciousness of the working class in America as well as in the rest of the world. Yet the most characteristic aspect of such novels escapes ideological definition completely, for it is a product of the age as it worked on writers beneath the level of consciousness of class or anything else. This is the *tone* of the Proletarian Novel: a note of sustained and self-satisfied hysteria bred on the one hand of Depression-years despair and on the other of the sense of being selected as brands to be snatched from the fire.

The Stalinist movement in the United States has always attracted chiefly marginal and urban groups; and if one thinks of the marginal and urban in the United States, he thinks, of course, largely of Jews. Especially in its cultural activities, in the John Reed Clubs, in the *New Masses* (and those cultural activities were of major importance in the thirties when the Communists captured few factories but many publishing houses), Jews participated in a proportion completely out of accord with their role in the total population. Indeed, the Movement was by way of being the typical strategy of the ambitious young Jew in a time of Depression for entering fully into American life. Jews who would have been dismayed by older kinds of bourgeois assimilation embraced this new method which allowed them at once to identify themselves with America and protest against certain aspects of its life.

Similarly, the intellectual, whether Jewish or not, found in the Movement an escape from the sense of alienation from American society which the twenties had brought to acute consciousness. One must realize the attractiveness of the orthodox Communist "culture" sponsored by the *New Masses* for the young man who was both an intellectual and a Jew. It is scarcely surprising that so many of them turned to the Proletarian Novel as their chosen form; even those who for aesthetic reasons found the genre unpalatable apologized for their apostasy, or tried to make up for it: like Nathanael West feeding his more orthodox contemporaries at the family hotel and boasting of having walked the picket line with James T. Farrell and Leane Zugsmith.

Still, no matter how alluring the Proletarian Novel might have been to the unproletarian Jewish writer, he could not, of course, write such a novel *as a Jew.* It was during the thirties, one remembers, that the Stalinists were officially condemning Jewish chauvinism in Palestine, and attacking Ludwig Lewisohn (who had entered his Zionist phase) as the blackest of reactionaries; and in those days, "race consciousness" was thought to be inimical to class consciousness. It is not surprising, after all, that a recent survey of the literature of the period, in a book called *The Radical Novel in America,* can point out only *one* Proletarian Novel which dealt specifically with anti-Semitism. This is a problem which must wait for the Popular Front novel and the Middlebrow Liberal Novel, which is to say, for the forties.

All of which does not mean, of course, that a Jewish writer could not *begin* with his Jewishness; and, as a matter of fact, Michael Gold's *Jews Without Money,* which appeared in 1930, was the prototype of the Proletarian Novel, going through eleven printings in its first year and setting a pattern for succeeding writers. Not quite a novel, really, or quite an autobiography, it seems more than anything a collection of vignettes of Jewish life making a moral point—a conversion tract illustrating the passage of a thinking man from Judaism to Communism. The pattern is simple enough (it is picked up and reinforced later in Isidor Schneider's *From the Kingdom of Necessity):* to make of "Jewish nationalism" and the Jewish religion the chief symbols of reaction; the pious man, the pillar of the synagogue, appears as a landlord and an owner of whorehouses; the rabbi becomes an old lecher; and the rituals of the Jews instances of hypocrisy and backwardness. The *Seder* (one thinks of what Herman Wouk will be doing fifteen years later to redeem all this!) an especial horror: "Ironical, isn't it? No people has suffered as the Jews have from the effects of nationalism and no people has held to it with such terrible intensity. . . ."

Can there be, then, in the American Jewish proletarian writer any Jewishness beyond a peculiarly Jewish self-hatred, a Jewish anti-Jewishness? To be sure, there is always available to him Jewish local color: the stumbling speech, the squalor, the joy peculiar to the Lower East Side or Brownsville; but these are by the thirties already sentimentalized clichés also available to the makers of Cohen and Kelly type movies. There is, beyond this, the constant awareness of alienation which belongs to the Jew: the sense of loneliness not as an accident but as a kind of chosenness; and in a writer like Gold the ancestral cry of *"Eli, Eli . . ."* persists. "In my ears still ring the lamentations of the lonely old Jews without money: 'I cash clothes, I cash clothes, my God, why hast thou forsaken me!' "

Not only has the concept of the choosing of all Israel in an election which seems an abandonment been transferred from the whole people to a part—to the poor alone—but in the process, what began as a mystery has become hopelessly sentimentalized. It is not for nothing that Mike Gold has been called the Al Jolson of the Communist Movement; indeed, in and through him, a cloying tradition of self-pity, which is also, alas, Jewish, and which had already possessed the American stage, moves on into literature. If the Communist Jewish writer can sing *"Eli, Eli . . ."* to his own tune, he can also sing *"A Yiddishe Mamme"* in a proletarian version. Here is Mike Gold once more: "My humble funny little East Side mother. . . . She would have stolen or killed for us. . . . Mother! Momma! I am still bound to you by the cords of birth. . . . I must remain faithful to the poor because I cannot be faithless to you."

All of this is secondary, however; the special meaning of Judaism for the radical writer of the thirties is, expectedly enough, its Messianism. "I believed," Gold writes, "the Messiah was coming, too. It was the one point in the Jewish religion I could understand clearly. We had no Santa Claus, but we had a Messiah." It is understandable, after all, that Marxism should feel at home with the Messianic ideal, since Marx seems to have envisaged himself, more often than not, as a prophetic figure: the last of the prophets promising a new heaven and a new earth. With the Russian Revolution, however, and the differentiation of Bolshevism, a new tone is apparent in Socialist messianism: a note at once apocalyptic and violent.

The old-fashioned sanity that characterizes Abraham Cahan is abandoned; and especially anything that smacks of the pacifism of the twenties is rejected in favor of an ideal of "hard Bolshevism" and class war. Two quite different sorts of feelings are involved, often confused with each other but logically quite separable: on the one hand, the desire, compounded of the self-hatred of the Jew and the self-distrust of the intellectual, that the good, clean, healthy workers of the future take over and destroy all that has come before them; on the other, an impulse to identify oneself with the future, to feel oneself for once strong and brutal and capable of crushing all that has baffled and frustrated one's dreams. "Oh workers' Revolution," Gold's protagonist cries out at the book's climax. "You brought hope to me, a lonely suicidal boy. You are the true Messiah. . . ."

Jewish American fiction in the thirties, whether specifically "proletarian" or not, is characterized by this frantic religiosity without God, this sense of the holiness of violence. Wherever one turns, there is the sense of a revelation, mystic and secular and terrible, as the only possible climax: the challenge to an unbelieved-in God to redeem Williamsburg at the end of Fuchs' first novel; the prayer to Pure Mathematics as a savior in Maurice Samuel's *Beyond Woman;* the invocation of the holy rage of John Brown in Leonard Ehrlich's *John Brown's Body;* the baffled and self-destructive attempt of Nathanael West's Miss Lonelyhearts to become Christ in a Christless world.

The Jewish novel of the twenties has as its typical theme assimilation and as its typical imagery the erotic; but the novel of the thirties is in theme and imagery, as well as politics, apocalyptic. Sex does not disappear from it completely, for the conquest of erotic taboos is a continuing concern of the contemporary novel; but its meaning and importance alike have been altered as compared with, say, *The Rise of David Levinsky* or Ben Hecht's *A Jew in Love.* From the Jew in love to the Jews without money of the thirties is a long way whose direction is indicated by Maurice Samuel's title *Beyond Woman.* Where erotic material does appear, it is likely to have the function which it assumes in Gold's book, to have become one more exhibit in the Chamber of Horrors: evidence of the evils of prostitution or the prevalence of the homosexual rape of small boys under Capitalism. More generally speaking, after Mike Gold, sex tends to be treated as just another sort of violence in a violent America.

In the 1930's, the Jewish-American novelists, like most of their Gentile fellows, become subscribers to the cult of violence, though for the Jewish writer such an allegiance has a special pathos because of the long opposition to violence in the Jewish inheritance. It is one more way of denying his fathers. And what could he do in any case? In those shabby, gray years, the dream of violence possesses the American imagination like a promise of deliverance. Politics is violent and apolitics equally so; whatever else a man accepts or denies, he does not deny terror.

Obviously, the thirties did not invent terror and violence in our fiction; as far back as our books go, there are images of horror: the torn corpse stuffed up the chimney; the skull split by a tomahawk; the whale spouting blood. Even a "funny book" like *Huckleberry Finn* has more corpses than anybody can ever remember. There are, however, two transformations in the thirties of the role and handling of violence.

The first is the *urbanization of violence;* that is to say, violence is transferred from the world of nature to the world of society, from what man must endure to what man has made. There is, of course, a special horror in considering the law of fang and claw walled in but unmitigated by the brick and glass of the city planners. Even a provincial writer like Faulkner is driven in those years to move into the city streets for images of terror adequate to the times; and *Sanctuary* remains of all his books the most appalling and Popeye, his sole urban protagonist, his most monstrous creation.

But the thirties mark the climax of an even more critical change: the ennobling of violence as "the midwife of history." Under the name of the Revolution, violence becomes not something to be fled, not the failing of otherwise admirable men, not a punishment for collective guilt—but the crown of social life. What had begun just after 1789 with the Terror and been hailed in America by the theoretically bloody Jefferson received in an age of mechanized warfare and mass production its final form. The lust for pain of Nietzsche and the hypostasizing of history by Hegel culminated in the twin horrors of Nazi and Soviet brutality; but a worse indignity had already been worked on the minds of intellectuals, conditioned in advance to accept one or the other.

In light of this, it is easy to understand that questions of ideology are secondary, that it is the pure love-fear of violence which distinguishes the novel of the thirties: a kind of passion not unlike that which moved the Germans before their final defeat, a desire for some utter cataclysm to end the dull-dragging-out of impotent suffering. Not only Communist-oriented writers produced such horror literature, but southerners like John Peale Bishop (in *Act of Darkness)* or Robert Penn Warren (in *At Heaven's Gate);* Hemingway made his obeisance to the mode in *To Have and Have Not;* and even so mild an upper-middlebrow traditionalist as James Gould Cozzens produced in *Castaway* a novella of the required shrillness.

In the official Communist version, the vision of the apocalypse is translated into that of the "Final Conflict" between worker and boss, Good and Evil; but this pat formula the better Jewish-American novelists could not quite stomach. Rather typically they temper the violence they cannot reject with humor, an ironic refusal to enter the trap completely. At the close of Daniel Fuchs' *Homage to Blenholt,* the three *shlemiels* who are his protagonists have reached the end of their illusions and are looking at each other in despair. One has come to realize that he will run a delicatessen for the rest of his life; another has come to see that the greatest event in his career will be winning three hundred dollars on a long shot.

> "Well," said Coblenz, "don't take it so hard. Cheer up. Why don't you turn to Communism?"
>
> "Communism?" cried Mrs. Balkin. "Listen to Mr. Bungalow. Communism!"
>
> "What has Communism got to do with it?" Munves sincerely wanted to know.
>
> "It's the new happy ending. You feel lousy? Fine! Have a revelation and onward to the Revolution!"

Fuchs' protagonists remain to the end victims and antiheroes, incapable of any catastrophe more tragic than the pratfall: but this is the traditional strategy of the comic writer. In a more complex way, Nathanael West and Henry Roth manage to achieve at once the antiheroic and the almost-tragic. In West, the comic butt is raised to the level of Everybody's Victim, the skeptical and unbelieved-in Christ of a faithless world; in Roth, the *shlemiel* is moved back to childhood, portrayed as the victim of circumstances he can never understand, only transcend.

West, of course, remains a humorist still; though in him humor is expressed almost entirely in terms of the grotesque, that is to say, on the borderline between jest and horror. In his novels, violence is not only subject matter; it is also technique, a way of apprehending as well as a tone and theme. Especially in the *Dream Life of Balso Snell,* one can see what West learned from the Surrealists during his stay in France: the violent conjunctions, the discords at the sensitive places where squeamishness demands harmony; the bellylaugh that shades off into hysteria.

Yet he is a peculiarly American case, too. In one of his few published critical notes he announces: "In America violence is idio-

matic, in America violence is daily." And it is possible to see him
as just another of our professional tough guys, one of the "boys in
the backroom" (the phrase is Edmund Wilson's—the title of a little
book in which he treated West along with John O'Hara). But West
is, despite his own disclaimers, in a real sense, a Jew. He is racked,
that is to say, by guilt in the face of violence, shocked and tor-
mented every day in a world where violence *is* daily. In *Miss Lonelyhearts,* he creates a kind of portrait of himself as one all nerves
and no skin, the fool of pity whom the quite ordinary horror of ordinary life lacerates to the point of madness. His protagonist is
given the job of answering "letters from the lovelorn" on a daily
newspaper and finds in this job, a "joke" to others, a revelation of
human misery too acute to bear.

But this is West's analogue for the function of the writer, whom
he considers obliged to regard unremittingly a suffering he is too
sensitive to abide; and in no writer is there so absolute a sense of
the misery of being human. He is child enough of his age to envision an apocalypse; but his apocalypse is a defeat for everyone. The
protagonist of *Miss Lonelyhearts* is shot reaching out in love toward a man he has (against his will) offended; the hero-*shlemiel* of
A Cool Million: or The Dismantling of Lemuel Pitkin goes from
one absurd anti-Horatio-Alger disaster to another, and after his
death becomes the hero of an American Fascist movement. But the
real horror-climax of his life and the book comes when, utterly
maimed, he stands on a stage between two corny comedians who
wallop him with rolled up newspapers in time to their jokes until
his wig comes off (he has been at one point scalped), his glass eye
falls out, and his wooden leg falls away; after which they provide
him with new artificial aids and begin again.

It is in *The Day of the Locust,* however, West's last book and
the only novel on Hollywood not somehow trivialized by its subject,
that one gets the final version of The Apocalypse according to Nathanael West. At the end of this novel, a painter, caught in a rioting
mob of fans at a Hollywood premiere, dreams, as he is crushed by
the rioters, his masterpiece, "The Burning of Los Angeles":

> Across the top he had drawn the burning city, a great bonfire of
> architectural styles. . . . Through the center . . . spilling into
> the middle foreground, came the mob carrying baseball bats

and torches—all those poor devils who can only be stirred by the promise of miracles and then only to violence, a great United Front of screwballs and screwboxes to purify the land. No longer bored, they sang and danced joyously in the red light of the flames.

West does not seem to be finally a really achieved writer; his greatness lies like a promise just beyond his last novel and is frustrated by his early death; but he is the inventor for America of a peculiarly modern kind of book whose claims to credence are perfectly ambiguous. One does not know whether he is being presented with the outlines of a nightmare endowed with a sense of reality or the picture of a reality become indistinguishable from nightmare. For the record, it must be said that the exploiters of such ambiguity are typically Jews: Kafka for the continent, West for us.

But in what sense is West a Jew at all? There is a violent flight from Jewish self-consciousness in his work; indeed, in *Balso Snell*, there is a bitter portrait of the kind of Jewish artist who feels obliged to insist on his origins:

> "Sirrah!" the guide cried in an enormous voice, "I am a Jew! and whenever anything Jewish is mentioned, I find it necessary to say that I am a Jew. I'm a Jew! A Jew!"

Indeed, whenever a Jew is directly identified in West, he is portrayed viciously enough to satisfy the most rabid anti-Semite; although one must hasten to add that this is balanced by portraits of anti-Semites which would gratify any Jew. Finally, however, anti-Semitism and anti-anti-Semitism do not really add up to Jewishness, much less cancel each other out. West's changed name is surely a clue; he is the first American Jewish writer to wear a name which is a disguise; the exact opposite of Henry Harland, first author of an American book with a Jewish milieu, who called himself Sidney Luska and tried to pass as a compatriot of his protagonists.

West, we are told, made a point of dressing in a Brooks Brothers suit, carrying a tightly rolled umbrella and going, conspicuously, on hunting trips—which is to say, he insisted in all ways on making himself the antitype of the conventional Jewish intellectual. Yet it seems to me inconceivable that anyone but an urban, second-generation Jew in revolt against his background could have produced the novels from *Balso Snell* to *The Day of the Locust*. Certainly, the epigram of C. M. Doughty, which he himself quotes, seems applicable to Nathanael West: "The Semites are like to a man sitting in a cloaca to the eyes, and whose brows touch heaven."

Henry Roth is quite another matter. *Call It Sleep*, which appeared in 1935, and which no one will reprint despite continuing critical acclaim, is a *specifically* Jewish book, the best single book by a Jew about Jewishness written by an American, certainly through the thirties and perhaps ever. Technically, Roth owes a great deal to James Joyce; and, indeed, it is the strategy of intense concentration on fragmented detail and the device of stream-of-consciousness (both learned from *Ulysses)* which protect his novel from the usual pitfalls of the ghetto book. He reverses the fatal trend toward long-winded chronicle, which had at once inflated and dimmed the portrayal of Jewish immigrant society from Abe Cahan's lifelong study of David Levinsky to Ludwig Lewisohn's "saga" of four generations. The events of *Call It Sleep* cover two years of ghetto life, from 1911 to 1913, and are funneled through the mind of a boy who is six at the start of the book. It is through the sensibility of this sensitive, poetic, mama-haunted, papa-hating Jewish child, full of fears and half-perceptions and misunderstandings, that the clichés of the form are redeemed to poetry.

But he serves another purpose, too, that of helping the author, apparently committed to the ends of the Movement, evade ideology completely. In the place of the Marxian class struggle, Roth sets an almost Dickensian vision of the struggle between the child and society, of the child as Pure Victim. The lonely boy and the hostile city make only the first in a series of counterpoints on which the book is based: the greenhorn and the American; a subtle and lovely Yiddish and a brutal, gray English; grossness and poetry; innocence and experience, finally Gentile and Jew. In a way, quite unexpected in the thirties, Roth plays off the values of the *Cheder* against the values of an outside world dedicated to a pagan hunger for sex and success.

The climax of the book comes when David, the young protagonist, thrusts the handle of a milk ladle down into a crack between streetcar rails and is shocked into insensibility. He has learned earlier of the power of the rails, when captured and tortured by a gang of Gentile hoods on the previous Passover, and has come somehow to identify that power with the coal of fire by which the mouth of Isaiah was cleansed. He feels the need of a similar cleansing, for young as he is, he has the sense of having played pander to his cousin Esther and a Gentile boy in order to be accepted in that boy's world. Just before he passes into complete unconsciousness, David is granted a vision—once more the apocalypse—in which all that troubles him is healed: his father's paranoiac rage and fear of cuckoldry; his mother's mute suffering and erotic fantasies; his own terrors and apostasies. Blended into his vision are the harsh cries of the street and the voice of a Socialist speaker prophesying the day on which the Red Cock will crow. For the vision, neither the eight-year-old David nor the author has a name; and as the boy falls from consciousness, he thinks: "One might as well call it sleep."

After this spectacular achievement, Roth wrote no more novels; he works now, one hears, in an insane asylum in upstate New York —and an occasional story reveals him still haunting his old material without conviction or power. It is not an untypical case in the history of American Jewish writers in the thirties. Gold and Schneider lapsed into mere pamphleteering: West and Fuchs moved off to Hollywood, where the former died; no promises were fulfilled. Looking back, one sees a series of apparent accidents and ideological cripplings, acts of cowardice and despair; and yet there is a sense that this universal failure is not merely the function of personal weakness but of a more general situation. Although all outward circumstances in the time of the Great Depression conspired to welcome the Jewish writer, the inward life of the Jewish community was not yet defined enough to sustain a major writer, or even to provide him with something substantial against which to define himself in protest.

3. Zion as Main Street

It is only during the past fifteen or twenty years that such a definition has been achieved. In this period, Jewish self-consciousness in

America has endured certain critical readjustments under pressure from world events: the rise and fall of Hitler; the consequent dissolution of virtually the whole European Jewish community; the establishment of the State of Israel, and the need to redefine the allegiance of American Jews as Jews and as Americans. Other less spectacular developments have exercised an influence, too: the closing off of mass immigration and the slow disappearance of Yiddish as a spoken language; the elimination of the "greenhorn" as a typical Jewish figure—all this accompanied by an increasing general prosperity for the majority of American Jews. No longer is our story that of the rise of an occasional David Levinsky, but that of almost the whole Jewish people on the march toward the suburbs; of the transformation of essential Jewish life into bourgeois life.

At the same moment, there has been a complementary entry of the Jews into the academic world. One reads with surprise and incredulity that when Ludwig Lewisohn graduated from Columbia, he was advised not to hope for a job teaching English anywhere in America. More and more these days, even in this sensitive Anglo-Saxon area, Jews have come to write and teach; and only the most unreconstructed backwoods anti-Semite is heard to murmur bitterly about men named Greenspan or Schwartzstein lecturing on Emerson or Thoreau. Jews, indeed, have come to control many of the positions of prestige in the intellectual world of America, as editors and journalists and lay critics as well as teachers and writers.*

We live at a time when there exists what can be called either a temptation or an opportunity, at any rate the possibility of Jews en-

---

* Only an occasional crackpot these days raises an unheard voice against the trend, as Mr. Jack Feltz (dealer in uranium property) protests in a recent mimeographed leaflet: "According to studies of . . . *Publishers' Weekly,* as high as one-third or more of many publishers' lists are the works of Jewish authors, while the Jewish people constitute something like one-thirtieth of our population. . . . The authorities of our literature are, chiefly, members of a minority group who . . . have their own especial bias and prejudice. Every book that goes into print . . . is either written by, edited by, advertised by, published by, or, what is common—all four— Jewish people. . . .

"Why are the works of degenerate authors declared 'Great American Writing,' when often they are in extremely poor English, and are demoralizing and dangerous to our youths? Is it not probable that literary careers are bought from these publishers, just as we would buy a box of soap at the supermarket? There is only one other possibility: these publishers are at war with the American intelligence, as well as its Christian morality."

tering fully into the suburban-exurban pattern of success, conformity, and acceptance in an America where right-minded citizens protest teaching *The Merchant of Venice,* and blatant anti-Semitism exists chiefly in the most backward elements of the working class and in the backwoods of the South. For better or for worse, the task of the Jewish-American novelist now is to give some sense of the settling down of Jews in our steam-heated, well-furnished *Galut* —or to struggle against it, if such a struggle is still possible.

For this reason, we are through with the traditional "up from the ghetto" kind of Jewish fiction as a living form. In such books as Alfred Kazin's *A Walker in the City,* Isaac Rosenfeld's *Passage from Home,* or *An End to Dying* by the very young writer Sam Astrachan, one sees attempts to redeem the old pattern; but such attempts seem finally nostalgic and vestigial—echoes of yesterday's concerns. What, then, is central and vital in the recent novel as written by American Jews? Perhaps the best way to begin to answer this is to consider the situation left by the collapse of the Proletarian Novel and the exhaustion of the messianic spirit.

Even before the end of the thirties, when the most aware began to feel that the post-World War I era was over and the pre-World War II era had already begun, proletarian fiction was officially liquidated. The Communist Party through its cultural organs began to prepare for the Popular Front Novel, for a kind of fiction *pious* rather than *apocalyptic* in its approach. No longer was intransigence the keynote, but cooperation; no longer were the "workers" the subject, but "the little people"; no longer was the *International* required mood music, but *America the Beautiful.* Sentimentality had replaced terror; and those who looked back longingly toward bloodier days were condemned as "infantile leftists."

Most crucial of all, the American Left, which had traditionally associated itself with the *avant-garde* in literature, turned away toward Hollywood and Broadway and nightclub folksingers from the Village. The concept of Art as a Weapon no longer led to old-fashioned Agitprop productions, but to slick creations provided by movie writers or Madison Avenue ad-men with bad consciences. The distinguished names, available in the thirties at least for petitions and pamphlets, Dreiser or Farrell or Dos Passos, began to be replaced by Rex Stout and Donald Ogden Stewart, Dashiell Hammett and Howard Fast.

Fast is particularly interesting as the last full-time bard of the Movement, its most faithful middlebrow servant in the arts. He has recently reached a final crisis of conscience and has made at last a public break with the Communist Party; but for some fifteen years beginning in 1942 he managed almost alone to create a kind of subliterature in tune with its changing political line. In *The Unvanquished* and *Citizen Tom Paine*, he found a way of adapting the historical novel to Stalinist uses, of making its sentimentality underwrite the pieties of "progressive politics," and thus broke out of the long silence which had followed the collapse of proletarian fiction. If he turned at last into the most dogged sort of formula writer, it was due only in part to his natural limitations. No one could have stood up long under the demand to redeem George Washington when "Americanism" becomes respectable; to refurbish Judah Maccabee when Judaism comes back into fashion; or to get Sacco and Vanzetti out of the mothballs when all else fails. That the official Popular Front hack be a Jew is in some ways ironical but not unexpected; for among the last faithful left to the Communists in America were certain Jews clinging to the ragged cliché that in the Soviet Union, at whatever price, anti-Semitism had been eliminated.

The accommodation of the Stalinist left to middlebrow pressures (and the more complicated adjustment of the anti-Stalinist left in the pages of *Partisan Review)* has left no place for the instinctively radical writer to turn. There is no more dismaying prospect than the loneliness and bewilderment of the belated apocalyptic writer, especially when he is too young for the experience of the thirties and has to make a secondhand, home-made version of class struggle fiction—out of G.I. platitudes and memories of Marxism. James Jones is, perhaps, the outstanding representative of the group; and Norman Mailer its chief Jewish proponent. In the latter's *The Naked and the Dead*, for instance, the Fascist villain out of a hundred weary Agitprop entertainments appears as General Cummings, surely one of the most improbable characters in all fiction.

Such writers, having no center, are provincials in the deepest sense of the word: that is to say, they repeat what they have never heard and invent all over again what is already worn out. Mailer is a case in point, recapitulating the whole recent history of literature before him: he rewrites the antiwar novel in *The Naked and the Dead*, the anti-Hollywood novel in *The Deer Park,* the novel of political disillusionment in *Barbary Shore.* Only the hectic sexuality, which threatens, despite his conscious intent, to replace politics completely, seems his own; the rest is unacknowledged (I suspect, unaware) quotation.

As in the writers of the thirties, in Mailer what remains of Jewishness is translated into social protest; though the chief rebels of his books are (like West's) almost pointedly *not* Jews. And yet in one sense, he is more the child of his sentimental times than he would be pleased to admit; certainly there appears for the first time in *The Naked and the Dead,* what is to become a standard character in the liberal-middlebrow war book: the Jewish Sad Sack. In Mailer's Goldstein, who finds the chief horror of war anti-Semitism in his own ranks, there is present in embryo Irwin Shaw's Noah Ackerman—and the protagonist of a score of movies to come.

Such lapses into the banal vocabulary of the middlebrows are, however, rare in Mailer. He may be clumsy and provincial, but he is above all things honest; and he refuses to endorse the clichés of enlightened liberalism. There is something healthy, I think, in preferring yesterday's platitudes to today's; for they are at least unfashionable, assurances that the writer is not merely on the make. Mailer is not, in any case, a typical figure, standing apart as he does from the two major developments which have followed the collapse of the Proletarian Novel.

Both these developments are of considerable importance for an understanding of Jewish writers in America since both are in large part products of Jewish writers, and both help to establish the background against which the later Jewish writer defines himself. The first development is a kind of literary Jacobinism: a resistance to the separation of radical politics and *avant-garde* art. Its adherents would reconstitute the alliance of antibourgeois social criticism and antibourgeois literary experiment; but this they would do outside of any party orthodoxy. The second is a species of literary liberalism which aims at rescuing Popular Front art, that is, self-righteous, middlebrow art, from the Communists in favor of an en-

lightened segment of the bourgeoisie. Let us consider them in reverse order.

The middlebrow liberal or liberal-colored fictionist responds to
the demands of a certain novel-reading section of the middle class
which would like to be Philistine in a really arty kind of way. Such
readers are more concerned with social problems than with art and
turn to novels merely as occasions for thinking about such "important problems." The kind of middlebrow fiction produced for their
benefit has established itself everywhere from *Good Housekeeping*
and the *Saturday Evening Post,* on the one hand, to the *New
Yorker,* on the other.

One of its newer subvarieties, science fiction, has opened up a
whole series of periodical and book-length markets. The first lower-
middlebrow form of fiction to challenge the long dominance of
the Western and the detective story, science fiction is in large part
a Jewish product. There are a score of Jewish writers among its
most widely read practitioners, as compared with practically none
among those of the two older types of institutionalized fantasy. The
basic myths of science fiction reflect the urban outlook, the social
consciousness, the utopian concern of the modern, secularized Jew.
The traditional Jewish Waiting-for-the-Messiah becomes in lay
terms the *commitment to the Future,* which is the motive force of
current science fiction. The notion of the Jewish cowboy is utterly
ridiculous, of a Jewish detective, Scotland Yard variety or private
eye, nearly as anomalous; but to think of the scientist as a Jew is almost tautological.

Much science fiction, set just before or after the Great Atomic
War still to come, embodies the kind of guilty conscience peculiar
to such scientist-intellectuals (typically Jewish) as Robert Oppen-
heimer; while the figure of Einstein presides over the whole New
Heaven and New Earth such literature postulates, replacing the
earlier Hebrew God who is—for most science fiction fans, certainly
—dead. Even in its particulars, the universe of science fiction is
born judaized; the wise old tailor, the absurd but sympathetic *yiddishe mamme* plus a dozen other Jewish stereotypes whiz un-
changed across in space and time. Even secret Jewish jokes are
made for the cognoscenti: the police on a corrupt, transgalactic
planet called in the exotic tongue of that world *Ganavim.* And in

the Superman comic books (lowbrow equivalent of science fiction) the same aspirations and anxiety are projected in the improbable disguise of the Secret Savior, bespectacled Clark Kent, who may look like a *goy* but who is invented by Jews. The biceps are the biceps of Esau, but the dialogue is the dialogue of Jacob.

The more "serious" middlebrow novel in form combines a clear narrative line (no confusing flashbacks or troublesome experiments in style) with a pious celebration of social protest in favor of Negroes, Jews, children of adulterous mothers, paraplegics, Hungarians—whatever is thoroughly unexceptionable and, of course, *up to date;* for such books must compete with the daily newspaper. In these works, a new, urban, professional, liberalized, and, I think, largely Jewish elite comes to terms with its own vague feelings of guilt at being so prosperous in a troubled world. The kind of people who learn all about their children from reading Gesell, who go to the Museum of Modern Art, who subscribe to *The Reporter,* who vote for Adlai Stevenson, also buy the novels of Budd Schulberg and Irwin Shaw to get the latest word on the "little people," with whom they sentimentally identify themselves.

Naturally enough, considering the strength of Jewishness in this group and the impact of Hitler on the whole newspaper-reading world, the first "little people" to be celebrated in the liberal novel were the "little Jews." Not only Jewish writers, but Jews and Gentiles alike, discovered at once this new form of the novel and the new subject (so ignored in the thirties) of anti-Semitism. Arthur Miller's first novel, *Focus,* Laura Z. Hobson's *Gentleman's Agreement,* Mary Jane Ward's *The Professor's Umbrella*—there is a whole stream of such books mounting to a kind of flood-peak with John Hersey's *The Wall.* They are profoundly sentimental in theme and tone and are written in the slickly finished style proper to a literary no man's land existing somewhere between Hollywood and Madison Avenue and blanketed with old copies of the *Saturday Review of Literature,* the *New Yorker* and the *Princeton Alumni Weekly.*

What is oddest about such fiction, however, is the way in which it is typically hoked-up; the books are never simply studies of anti-Semitism in action, they are studies of anti-Semitism with a gimmick. Miller, for instance, deals with a man who, though a Gentile, *looks* like a Jew when he puts on glasses and is persecuted when his eyes fail. Mrs. Hobson's book is about a reporter who *pretends* he is a Jew and brings down upon himself the discrimination of anti-Semites. It is not only a certain middlebrow ideal of form which demands the gimmick, but a basic uncertainty which is aptly symbolized by such a tricky device. What, after all, *is* a Jew in this world where men are identified as Jews only by mistake, where the very word becomes merely an epithet arbitrarily applied? It is difficult to make a novel about anti-Semitism when one is not sure exactly what, beside being the butt of anti-Semites, makes a man a Jew.

There are, to be sure, occasional portraits of real Jews beside the imaginary ones; but the former are such monsters of humility and gentleness and endurance and piety that it is impossible to believe in them. Such protagonists are no more real than the happy endings which await them: reconciliations in an atmosphere of goodwill even less credible than the atmosphere of exaggerated hostility with which such fables typically begin. The pattern is set once and for all in a story by Irwin Shaw called "Act of Faith," in which a young man, scared by his father's accounts of anti-Semitism at home, decides to keep as insurance a Luger he has picked up on the battlefield. He thinks, however, of his wartime buddies, "of all the drinks they had had together, and the long marches together, and all the girls they had gone out with together" and decides to sell the pistol after all. "Forget it," he says finally, "what could I use it for in America?" What begins as a political problem (touched with hysteria) is solved as a sentimental one (touched with politics).

From a story of anti-Semitism to one of the war is an easy jump; indeed, the liberal war novel is only one more species of the high-minded literature of social reform: a subvariety, in the hands of Jewish writers in particular, of the novel of anti-Semitism. Shaw's *The Young Lions* is the prime example of the genre, anticipations of which we have already noticed in Mailer's *The Naked and the Dead*. In a fundamental sense, there is nothing *new* in such novels; they do not change the protest form of the war-book invented just after World War I; but the method has been perfected: the tone of superficial realism set by unflinching descriptions of death, rape, and the other usual calamities of combat; the rejection of certain more obvious stereotypes of the enemy, and the exploitation of others: the reactionary American General, for instance, but especially the "representative platoon," with the Jewish Sad Sack to help make up its roster.

One raised entirely on such literature and the movies based on their clichés would believe the United States Army to be carefully organized so that each platoon contains a pure, sentimental sample of the "little people" at war: a cocky, slight Italian, a Brooklyn Jew, a raw-boned, blond farm boy, etc. Certainly, no such group would dare set off without its Jew, the kind of understanding victim who, in the recent liberaloid film *Attack,* is portrayed as reciting *Kaddish* for a Catholic thug who dies while trying to reach a gun and kill (naturally!) an evil officer.

Shaw's Jew is Noah Ackerman, a self-educated intellectual, hated at first by his buddies, in part because a copy of *James Joyce* is found in his footlocker, but later much admired after offering to fight the six or eight toughest men in his platoon. In him, we meet the stereotyped antistereotype of the Jew: since the old stereotype makes the Jew a coward, he is brave; since it makes the Jew a war-resister, he is a combat hero; since it makes the Jew an enemy of personal violence, he is (for quite high-minded reasons) dedicated to it. What Hemingway had satirized as overcompensation in Robert Cohn is here glorified.

There are, however, two other major characters in *The Young Lions* beside the Jew as Fighting Sad Sack: the antistereotype stereotyped Nazi and an enlightened, sensitive American who has passed from Broadway to the front and is the eye of the book. The Nazi is permitted to kill the Jew, but Michael Whiteacre, the emissary from the world of Popular Culture, kills the Nazi. This is all quite satisfactory to the readers; for Michael is clearly intended to be their representative in the action: a projection of the mind for which Shaw is writing, the social group for which he speaks.

His work fulfills the ideal proposed to himself by the bureaucratized intellectual dreaming of what he would do if released by Hollywood or the T.V. network. *The Young Lions* is, one remembers, the book which the gigolo-scriptwriter in *Sunset Boulevard* (and presumably the scriptwriter behind him) reads in his spare time.

Budd Schulberg is, of course, another novelist who speaks for the same audience; and his *What Makes Sammy Run?* is as appropriate a representation of the Hollywood novel on the middlebrow level as *The Young Lions* is of the war novel (or, indeed, as Schulberg's own *On the Waterfront* of the liberaloid labor story).

When Schulberg's earlier book appeared, there was much pointless and confusing comment on the presumably anti-Semitic implications of his portrayal of Sammy Glick—as if this were the first portrait of an evil Jew to have appeared in American literature. In the midst of such properly middlebrow polemics, most readers failed to notice the more unforgivable travesties of Jews in Schulberg's noble scriptwriters, who read Silone's *Fontamara* in *their* spare moments and fought the good fight for the Screenwriters' Guild despite blacklisting and redbaiting.

Schulberg's novel, like all sentimental melodramas, splits into opposing symbolic characters what in fact exists in one contradictory soul. Once understood in this light, the book may be read as a portrait of the artist as a Hollywood employee: that is, a writer like Schulberg (and Shaw) is in part the noble Jewish supporter of the Loyalists and trade-unionism, but in part, too, Sammy Glick, the poor boy on the make. They, too, are sons of a first generation of immigrants which had destroyed itself for their sake in a strange world; they, too, are eager to be heard, to be effective, to be successful—and to break out of the trap of a stereotyped Jewishness without money. They are more complicated men, to be sure, than Sammy Glick; but then everyone is: even Herman Wouk.

Wouk's work does, however, possess a certain importance for revealing on a less sophisticated level ambitions analogous to those which inform *What Makes Sammy Run?* and *The Young Lions.* If Shaw and Schulberg can be said to speak for the mass entertainers with yearnings to transcend their world, Wouk can be understood as representing the ad writers and gag writers who are convinced that the same slick techniques by which they earn their livings can do justice to certain modest liberal values, and that those values are compatible with the suburban lives they lead. Turning from Shaw and Schulberg to Wouk, one notices certain differences: less shock, fewer dirty words, less stylistic pretension. His is a world that cries

"Keep it clean!" and the one thing that that world finds dirtier than four-letter words is highbrow art.

A common sentimentality, however, binds them together and a common store of stock "little people." Greenwald, the Jew of Wouk's war novel, *The Caine Mutiny,* is blood brother to the Ackerman of Shaw's *The Young Lions:* both are Jews who face up to Gentile versions of courage and honor which exclude them, not by challenging those codes but by aping them; both attempt to prove, despite the handicaps of a Jewish physique and a long tradition of nonviolence, that they can outdrink and outfight any *goy.* But Greenwald has adapted to the world that surrounds him even more shamelessly than Ackerman, having neither a taste for James Joyce nor a principled distrust of the armed forces. The villainous intellectual who does is called Keefer and is clearly (thank God!) not a Jew.

The reconciliation which Wouk demands goes far beyond the embracing of one's fellow yahoos in battle camaraderie as advocated by Shaw. It requires embracing the whole military, the whole social order in all its smug security, because, as Greenwald reminds especially his Jewish readers, it was Captain Queeg who kept mama out of the Nazis' soap dish. "Captain Queeg, yes, even Queeg and a lot of sharper boys than any of us. Best men I've ever seen. You can't be good in the Army or Navy unless you're goddam good, though maybe not up on Proust and *Finnegans Wake* and all." *The Stars and Stripes Forever* blend with *A Yiddishe Mamme,* as Gold had once blended the latter with the *International*—and the way is clear for Marjorie Morningstar.

Marjorie is, indeed, our new middlebrow muse, translated from Wouk's book to the cover of *Time* to the movies with scarcely a pause for breath: a portrait of accommodation as the young girl. That she is Jewish is the final touch: a tribute to the triumph of liberalism in the suburbs, the truce with anti-Semitism of the American middle class, and the end of surly intransigeance among the Jews. In the form of Noel Airman, Wouk has isolated all that is skeptical, anti-Philistine, and indifferent to bourgeois values in the Jewish-American tradition; and Airman he has made his villain. With him he identifies everything that stands between the Jew and social acceptance, the novelist and popularity; with Marjorie he identifies all that makes the Jew acceptable and the Jewish novelist a best-seller. It is one of the melodramatic fissions like the one we have noticed in Shaw and Schulberg; though this time the author isolates and casts out of himself symbolically not his greed for success but all that stands between him and that success.

What is truly strange is not that Marjorie should seem representative to the bourgeois Jewish community, but that she should also strike the American community at large as a satisfactory image. Yet it is comprehensible in the end that the enlightened American *allrightnik,* Gentile or Jew, should find in the suburban Jewish housewife the proper symbol of interfaith "tolerance," the vision of unity in diversity possible where no one any longer believes in anything but the hundred-per-cent Americanism of just believing.

This is not yet, however, a total picture of the middlebrow novel as written by the Jewish American writer. If Shaw defines the middle of the middle, and Wouk its lower limits, it is J. D. Salinger who indicates its upper reaches. Though Salinger has written always for the circle of middlebrow periodicals that includes *Good Housekeeping* and the *New Yorker,* he has maneuvered constantly (though at first almost secretly) to break through the limits of that circle. He has piously acknowledged in his stories the standard ritual topics of the enlightened bourgeoisie: the War and anti-Semitism; but he has been concerned underneath with only a single obsessive theme: the approach to madness and the deliverance from it, usually by the intervention of a child. His "little people" are often quite literally little, usually small girls; and his favorite protagonists are under twenty, their typical crisis the last pre-adult decision of deciding whether or not to remain in school.

The themes that find full expression in *Catcher in the Rye* are tried early in short magazine fiction. In "A Girl I Know," there first appears the familiar, six-foot-two, blackhaired boy, cast out of school; though in this case he is eighteen, has been expelled from college, and finds his way to Austria where he becomes involved in a brief, utterly innocent love affair with a Jewish girl, who can speak no more English than he can German. The War separates them, and he returns to Europe to find her dead, killed by Nazis. In the much-reprinted "For Esme with Love and Squalor" the other half of the obsessive fable is sketched in: the story of a man redeemed from a combat breakdown by a gift from an orphaned, twelve-year-old, upper-class girl, with whom he has had a brief tea-table conversation in England.

In *Catcher in the Rye,* the blackhaired boy on the lam from school and the man threatened with insanity are joined together; the savior becomes the little sister—and the sentimental-political background is sloughed away in favor of a discreetly hinted-at world of religious implications. One has the sense that Salinger is making a real bid to break out of the trap of middlebrow "understanding" into the realm of the tragic; but the attempt fails. It is impossible to believe in Holden Caulfield finally, for he is too unreal, a creature of tricks of style, set against an utterly unconvincing family background. One knows that he is intended to represent a holy innocent against whom the rest of the world is measured: a kind of prep-school, upper-income-bracket Huckleberry Finn, who cannot quite light out for the Territory but is redeemed by a little girl in a climax essentially sentimental; yet he ends as the prep-school boy's dream of himself, a slickly amusing model imitated by a hundred seventeen-year-olds in a score of secondary-school magazines from coast to coast.

In "Zooey," a recent novella published in the *New Yorker,* Salinger seems to me to have recast his story, so often unsuccessfully attempted, in much more convincing form. If "Zooey" moves us where *Catcher in the Rye* merely amuses, it is because for once the madness of the theme is allowed to break up the slickness of the style; and the family tragedy which is Salinger's essential theme is uncontaminated by required subject matter, erotic or political, essentially alien to him. The only romance to which he really responds is the family romance: Orestes saved from the furies by Electra (though this time he has reversed the roles); and he has brought his myth in all purity *home,* to his own Manhattan and to the Jewishness with which he has had so much trouble coming to terms. His protagonists may find their final peace in a religious revelation compounded of Zen Buddhism and Christian mysticism; but they begin at least in a Jewish milieu (half-Jewish only, he insists) of quiz kids and memories of the Pantages circuit. Salinger seems to

me by all odds the most interesting of the middlebrow writers, torn
between a professional knowledge of what is permitted the entertainer and a desire to surrender all striving to the attainment of a
mystic's peace. The assertion at the end of "Zooey" that the Fat
Lady of the middling audience is "Christ Himself. Christ Himself,
buddy!" seems to me one of the wackiest and most winning attempts to compromise these contradictory impulses.

The second major direction of recent fiction, what I have called
earlier the Jacobin protest, is a last attempt to maintain the snobbism of the highbrow in a world which undercuts his existence. It is
associated, in its Jewish manifestations at least, with *Partisan Review* and the publications that flank it: *Commentary, Encounter,*
and the *New Leader,* on the one hand; *Kenyon Review, Sewanee
Review,* and certain other literary quarterlies, on the other. It is not
especially relevant from our point of view that *Partisan* was originally political in nature, pledged to retaining the purity of Marxism
at a time when the official Communist movement was in retreat toward Popular Frontism; what *is* important is that it was pledged
also to maintain against the bourgeoisie the alliance of high art and
radical thinking.

By the 1950's as a matter of fact, Marxism had become a memory, a special condition of their youth, to most of *Partisan Review*'s
remaining collaborators; respectability crept inexorably in upon it.
At various points, indeed, certain super-Jacobins left the magazine's pages in despair. Not the least interesting of these is Paul
Goodman, who wanted to maintain an uncompromised allegiance
to pure bohemianism and nonaccommodation. He is at present a
lay analyst, influenced in his practice by the teachings of Wilhelm
Reich; and his concern with depth psychology helps shape his fiction, which is also based in part on the techniques of Kafka and the
devices of Yiddish folk humor.

Yet even those who remain and have most blatantly accommo-
dated to the world around them still share something with further
dissenters like Goodman, something which separates them clearly
from the middlebrow writers we have been discussing. What is it
that they share beneath all their differences? I have called it earlier
the snobbism of the highbrow; and their enemies are likely to label
it "negativism." Perhaps it is best thought of as a sort of vestigial,

spiritual Trotskyism: an obligation to the attitudes of dissent which survives the ideological grounds for dissent. It arises in any case from their early conditioning in endless polemics on Marxian theory and their exposure from adolescence on to Freudian concepts; and makes them more closely kin in certain ways to European intellectuals than to more traditional American writers.

Perhaps most important of all is the fact that such writers possess in common a brand of experience which is rich and suggestive. They are urban; they are second-generation Americans; they are men and women whose adolescence and early youth came between the Great Wars, was influenced by the Civil War in Spain, and haunted by the Depression; they remain strangers in the world of prosperity in which they now, quite comfortably, live. They are joined to each other and separated from the rest of their generation by the experience of having accepted and rejected Communism.

They are, finally, typically Jewish: secularized, uncertain Jews in most cases to be sure; but in all cases possessed by the ghosts of their Jewish past; and they continue to wrestle with the lay messianism which was the gift of that past to them. Their peculiar relationship to their Jewishness emphasizes their sense of alienation (it is a favorite word of theirs, very annoying but inescapable), and protects them against the Wouk-Shaw-Schulberg kind of simpleminded, liberal-middlebrow accommodation.

Yet the blessing which has fallen upon Wouk has also been bestowed (even more fantastically) upon *Partisan Review*. For better or for worse, the time has come when each cultural level in America looks to some Jewish-sponsored myth for a justification of its existence and its dreams; for some the Superman of the comics, for some the moralistic robots of Isaac Asimov, for some Marjorie Morningstar, for some images of urban alienation out of the pages of *Partisan Review*. Certainly, that magazine despite the tininess of its actual subscription list exercises at home and abroad a fantastic influence. If the concept of the highbrow has become for most Americans associated with the notion of the urban, Jewish, former Communist, this is in part the work of *Partisan Review*.

Certainly, as far as literature is concerned, it has introduced over the past fifteen years a group of writers rivaled in their variety and the richness of their common themes only by the Southern group which includes Eudora Welty, Carson McCullers, etc. Among them are writers like Delmore Schwartz, who has not yet produced a novel, but who has, in the short stories collected in *The World Is a Wedding,* managed to evoke the tone and texture of second generation life in America better than anyone I know. To render an undramatized sense of gray people in gray cities, speaking to each other in gray voices and gray words, he has evolved a desperately flat style, which, when it does not succeed, can be boring beyond belief; but which, when it works, carries an unparalleled conviction. There are further the *Partisan Review* adaptors of Kafka, in particular Isaac Rosenfeld, who made in his short stories something new and disturbing of Kafkaesque ambiguity and grotesque humor and who pushed forward the possibilities of Kafkaesque form, the symbolic statement neither quite essay nor quite story.

There is, finally, Bernard Malamud, recipient of one of the *Partisan Review* fellowships in fiction, who is presently enduring an astonishingly universal acclaim, the latest manifestation of the hunger among American readers for occasions to identify with Jewish life. Though his shorter work has appeared chiefly in *Partisan and Commentary,* he is much less political than most of his fellow contributors, free of their (in some cases obsessive) concern with the aftermath of the Communist experience. Close to forty-five, he is only now coming into full possession of his talent and his subject matter, and so has avoided the typical *Partisan Review*-ers' experience of being twice-born, once as a Bolshevik, once as a human. Yet he emerges from the same milieu as his more political colleagues, trades like them (though more fantastically) on the vestiges of urban Jewishness, on the kind of American experience closest to the moral life of Europe. His first novel, *The Natural,* dealt improbably enough with a baseball player (last symbol for the city-dweller of the heroic), handling a symbolic story with gusto and tact. His second book, *The Assistant,* more conventionally centered upon the family of a poor Jewish shopkeeper in the thirties, but ended, quite astonishingly for all its matter-of-fact tone, with the circumcision of its Italian protagonist; a desperate Happy Ending! It is all as if Mike Gold had never existed. Malamud did not, however, really arrive until the publication of his collected short stories (in a volume called *The Magic Barrel),* whose discreet flirtation with sentimentality perhaps made their acceptance easier. These stories tell and retell a fable in which a scholarly, timid, or genteel protagonist, secure or on the verge of security, confronts some seedy, living projection of the lostness and terror which his life denies—some more ultimate Jew; and we come away with the conviction that Malamud remains as a writer (thank God!) a good deal blacker, more *demonic* than he is ever prepared to admit—even to himself.

Malamud's meaning seems to me to be still defining itself and his significance to belong to what lies ahead, unlike that of the two major figures of the last decade to whom I now come. The first is Lionel Trilling, who is to me an endlessly fascinating case, though finally, I fear, a disappointing one. Indeed, the clue to his fascination lies in the last-minute failure of what is a complex and subtle sensibility; in the fact that as a fictionist, he doesn't quite work. Yet he was willing to attempt in *The Middle of the Journey* the novel which some writer of his kind must someday achieve: the story of the allure of Communism and of the disillusion with it. Norman Mailer has tried his hand at it, to be sure, but without having quite lived through the experience, and Isaac Rosenfeld has explored it a little obliquely in one short story; while Leslie Fiedler has endlessly circled around it in his shorter fiction. Only Trilling has made the full-scale attempt; and it is perhaps a certain air of schematism in his approach, a sense of his having reached this item on a list of Important Things to be Done, which mars the book.

The events of the novel, at any rate, finally remain unconvincing, both on the symbolic level (despite their relationship to the central experience of a generation) and on the literal one (despite their resemblance to the newspaper story of Hiss and Chambers); because they come to us refracted through the mind of a singularly unconvincing protagonist, a kind of cross between Matthew Arnold and E. M. Forster, caught at the moment of his entry into middle age and at the point of recovery from a wasting disease. He is both genteel and Gentile, this Laskell, through whom the working-class characters of the book become caricatures and its passion merely literary—not Trilling, of course, but a mask Trilling prefers to assume, a mask of the bourgeois academic who is beyond Judaism as he is beyond the clichés of middlebrow liberalism. I do not know whether Trilling lacks vitality because of his failure to tap his own Jewish sources, or whether he fails to tap those sources because of an initial lack of vitality; but somewhere here there is a clue to his failure, a failure whose outward symbol is the lack of Jewish major protagonists in a novel by a Jew about an experience deeply rooted in Jewish life.

He is much more successful in certain short stories, in "Of This Time, of That Place" and "The Other Margaret," where he can concentrate on a narrower world of university-oriented, genteel, New York, middle-class culture, in which Jewishness survives chiefly as what used to be called "ethical culture," a kind of diffuse moral concern. When he enters the larger world of the novel and confronts in particular the absurdity essential to the Communist experience in America, he is defeated by the very talents which make him so much at home in the world of late nineteenth-century British fiction.

Saul Bellow is quite another matter. The Author of *The Dangling Man, The Victim, The Adventures of Augie March* and a recent collection of shorter fiction called *Seize the Day,* he is already an established writer; although in the annoying fashion of American journalism (he is after all younger than Faulkner or Hemingway) he is still referred to as a "young novelist." Looking at the whole body of his work, one has the sense of a creative restlessness, an adventurousness, which distinguishes him quite sharply from such other established fictionists as Trilling, on the one hand, or Irwin Shaw, on the other. Even such younger, dissident middlebrows as Herbert Gold seem beside him to lack technical courage and real commitment.

Bellow can, on occasion, mute his style as he has done in *The Victim* and in the novella which gives his most recent collection its name; but even under wraps, his language has a kind of nervous life, a tough resiliency unequaled by any other American Jewish writer of the moment. Perhaps the fact that Yiddish was his first language has something to do with the matter; but when he unleashes his fancy and permits himself a kind of rich, crazy poetry based on the juxtaposition of high language and low, elegance and slang, I am reminded of *Moby Dick*. The dialogue of his books possesses a special vitality; he can report a passage of conversation about ideas which leaves one feeling that his characters have exchanged more than words, have really touched each other as with a blow or a kiss.

In the body of his work, the ideas of the *Partisan Review* group (it does not matter how far he thinks he has left them behind) come fully alive in literature for the first time; they exist, that is to say, as they existed at their best in the minds of the men who held them; for those men at their best *lived* such ideas and did not merely believe them. Not only does Bellow have a style more vigorous than that of Trilling; but he moves in a world which is larger and richer and more disorderly and delightful—a world which he calls most often Chicago, though it is the externalization of fancy as well as memory. Implicit from his beginnings is the impulse toward the picaresque, which broke free finally in the sprawling, episodic shapelessness of *Augie March*—whose very formless form protests the attempt to impose tight, aesthetic patterns upon a world whose essence is chaos.

Bellow is, not unexpectedly in an age when writers in general have entered the university and Jews in particular have found a home there, a teacher like Trilling. The Jim Tully ideal of the author-bum, still played at by novelists like Nelson Algren, has never had much appeal for the Jewish writer in America; but though Bellow rejects the mask of the hobo bard, he does not assume that of the cultured humanist. His myth of himself is not that of the morally discriminating bourgeois at home over cocktails; but of the lonely city-dweller moving among boarding houses and cheap hotels, shabby restaurants and gray city streets in the heat of midsummer. The typical Bellow protagonist is the man whose wife has left him or has gone off to her mother's, the man returning to a house in disorder.

He is the person who, all amenities stripped away, feels himself stripped to his human essence. And the human essence, the naked fact of a man in a Bellow book is never an answer but always the question: What am I, after all? What, after all, is man? To which the unpromising answer is returned: You are what asks; go on asking. Here is Bellow's true center as well as what makes him central for all of us; he has realized not more clearly, perhaps, but more passionately than anyone what the collapse of the Proletarian Novel really meant: not the disappearance only of a way of writing, never very fruitful in any case, but also the dissolution of the last widely shared definition of man—as victim or beneficiary of the social order.

Because Bellow does not subscribe to the liberal's illusion that the definition of the human in social terms is still viable; because he knows that Man, in the old sense, is dead—he is able to redeem all the typical books of the middlebrow-liberal canon. *The Dangling Man* is his book about the war; *The Victim,* his novel of anti-Semitism; *Augie March,* his examination of the perils of success; *Seize the Day,* his fable of failure in a world of prosperity—his own *Death of a Salesman.* But in each, ambiguity has replaced sentimentality, the tragic or the joyous displaced self-congratulation and self-conscious piety. The Jew and the anti-Semite, the machiavellian and the *shlemiel* come alike to the same revelation.

It is because he manages to exact from the most unpromising material the stubborn vision of lonely man in a world which no longer provides his definition that Saul Bellow is able at last to create the most satisfactory character ever projected by a Jewish writer in America: Augie March. With the book itself, shrill, repetitious, in spots hysterically euphoric, I have certain quarrels; with Augie, none. He is an image of man at once totally Jewish, the descendant of the *schemiels* of Fuchs and Nathaniel West, and absolutely American—the latest avatar of Huckleberry Finn. In him, there are blended in perfect irony those twin, incompatible American beliefs: that the answer is just over the next horizon and that there is no answer at all.

It is, I think, the final commentary on our age and on the place the Jew occupies in its imagination, that Huck Finn, when he returns to our literature not as an item of nostalgia but as an immortal archetype, returns without his overalls, his fishing pole and his freckles, as a Chicago kid making his way among small-time Jewish machiavellians. More was needed, however, than the age; the moment demanded a Jewish hero, perhaps, but hesitated indifferently between Augie March and Marjorie Morningstar. What was demanded was the talent and devotion and conviction which belong particularly to Bellow, and the rich, complicated milieu out of which he has emerged.

Missoula, Montana
—1959

SEVEN

The Image of Newark
and the Indignities of Love:
Notes on Philip Roth*

IN RECENT years, I have more often gone by Newark than into it, though it is the place where I was born and brought up. Still, seeing even from the Pulaski Skyway the Public Service Building lifted above the Meadows, and imagining around it the yellow trolley buses and the crowds at the curbs, frantic and disheveled as refugees—I feel again the ennui and terror and crazy joy of my childhood. It was at once depressing and exciting to live in a place which we came slowly to realize did not exist at all for the imagination. That Newark was nowhere, no one of us could doubt, though it was all most of us knew. What history the city possessed had been played out before our parents or grandparents were a part of it, and we did not even trouble to tell ourselves that we disbelieved it. What could Robert Treat, the founding father, mean to second generation Jewish boys living on a street of two-and-a-half-family houses with stone lions on the stoops? He was an embossed figure on a teaspoon, steeple-hatted and unreal: a souvenir given away at a forgotten centennial and fought over by the kids when the pot roast was taken off the table and the stewed fruit brought on.

And Newark itself, the whole living city, what was it beyond a tangle of roads defining our own neighborhood and enclosing others

---

* Originally a review of *Goodbye, Columbus.*

utterly alien? The city on whose streets we walked with school-
books or ice cream cones or packages from the store we could not
feel for a moment as one of those magical centers whose very
names were thrilling to say: Paris, London, even New Orleans or
Chicago or New York—the last only ten miles away. Newark was
not even a joke like Brooklyn or Oshkosh or Peoria; vaudeville performers with canned gags for everywhere on the circuit could
scarcely find one able to extort a perfunctory laugh. In those days,
to be sure, there were the Bears, a ball club at least, and always the
airport; after a while Dutch Schultz was shot in a local tavern, and
for a thrilling moment Longie Zwillman, whose mother we could
watch walking our sidewalks with the diamonds he bought her,
made the Public Enemy list! Public Enemy Number One, we liked
to boast; but I have been afraid to try to verify it, uneasily aware
that at best he was only third or fourth.

No, even as kids we felt really how undefined, how character-
less our native place was—without a legend older than last week's
Star-Eagle. We did not *know* its characterlessness, perhaps, but we
lived it just as we lived its ugliness. Later we would know, when it
was time. In the meanwhile, we prepared for the moment of knowledge by reading in that Public Library, in which, fittingly, the protagonist of Philip Roth's longest story works to put himself through
college. If Newark, our Newark, had any focal point at all it was
The Library; but there those of us who took books seriously
learned almost first of all that poor Newark had no writer, and
hence no myth to outlive its unambitious public buildings, its mean
frame houses. When Bamberger's Department Store was at last
closed down and the Prudential Insurance Company had crumbled
away, how would anyone learn that we had ever existed? Maybe
the name would survive at least on some old commutation ticket for
the Hudson Tubes, petrified in coal dust.

There was, to be sure, Stephen Crane, memorialized in the
classroom, but his fictional world was a small-town Gentile world
called Whilomville, not his native Newark at all; and we found it as
alien as most of the teachers who told us about it—or as those
Newark *goyim* who are all the time passing by the centers of action
of Roth's stories without ever quite impinging on them: the *shikses*
in white hats, the Sunday churchgoers walking to and from scarcely

conceivable services. For Newark, *our* Newark, to exist for the imagination of strangers and of our own children, Newark would have to produce a writer as vulgar, comical, subtle, pathetic, and dirty as itself. He would have to be Jewish, un-genteel, emancipated from all limitations except those of memory and of the remembered city.

But by the mid-fifties, it was clearly too late for such a writer to appear. With prosperity, the city we had known, the city of *cheders* and lox, "Vote Communist" buttons and college boys working in shoestores, despair in gravel schoolyards and epiphanies in the open stacks, had long since disappeared. A prosperity more final than death had translated the very *yentes* from the brick stoops to the Beach Clubs of Livingston and even more unimaginable suburbs; had removed the sons of leatherworkers and the owners of candy stores to Bucknell or Ohio State or (God forbid!) Princeton. Those who had not lusted for the suburbs or college towns had dreamed of New York; and to each the best he could desire was granted. The houses, the lots, the hedges that had defined our Newark passed now into the possession of the Negroes, from whose midst the laureate would have to come that we had apparently not been able to bring to birth. At best, our Newark would be in the long life of the city, multiple and squalid as Troy's, the Newark *before* the Newark that had become a fact of literature; archaeologists would give us the proper number.

In Philip Roth's stories, however (how can he be only twenty-six?), my own remembered and archaic city survives, or more precisely, lives fully for the first time; I live fully for the first time the first twenty years of my life. Maybe he has only dreamed that world, reconstructed it on the basis of scraps of information recollected from conversations with cousins or older brothers or uncles; or maybe a real city only becomes a mythic one when it is already dead. No matter—he has dreamed truly. In his nightmare vision, that is, a Newark very like the one from which I still occasionally wake sweating has been rescued from history, oddly preserved. At the Little Theatre across the Park from the Museum, Hedy Lamar is still playing in *Ecstasy,* as she played for 39 weeks (or was it 79?) when I was sixteen. Through the landscape of "switchman's shacks, lumberyards, Dairy Queens, and used-car lots," Roth's

characters still ascend the one hundred and eighty feet toward suburban coolness—the breath of air of which Newarkers vainly
dream all summer long. For it is summer, of course, Newark's infernal season, in Mr. Roth's fictional city—and somebody's aunt
and uncle are "sharing a Mounds bar in the cindery darkness of
their alley, on beach chairs." It is possible to persuade oneself
(though Roth does not say so) that with the proper coupon clipped
from the Newark Evening News one could still get *three* transpar-
ent White Castle Hamburgers for a nickel.

I would not have believed I could feel nostalgia for the meager
world Roth so improbably evokes, and I do not really believe it
now; but there is a suspicious kind of satisfaction for me in knowing that world is fixed now forever in his gray authentic poetry. I
can smell the sweat of my own lost August nights as I read *Goodbye, Columbus,* and am aware that I must be on guard lest, sentimentally and uncharacteristically (God knows!), I go out to meet
Philip Roth more than halfway. I realize that because there is more
Newark in the title piece of his book—more passionate social an-
thropology, rich as invention, depressing as fact, witty as the joke
the survivors of Newark have had to make of their lives to live so
long—it is for me the most moving of Roth's fictions. But I am
convinced that my reaction is more than personal and eccentric.

There is more room in his single novella than in any of his shorter
stories for nontheoretical life, for the painful wonder of what is
given rather than the satisfactory aptness of what is (however skill-
fully) contrived to substantiate a point. Random and inexhaustible,
such life is, after all, more the fictionist's business than any theme,
even the rewardingly ironic and surely immortal one of how hard it
is to be a Jew—quite differently elaborated in "Defender of the
Faith," and "Eli the Fanatic." For the first, Philip Roth has already
received the young Jewish writer's initial accolade: the accusation
of anti-Semitism; and both stories are effective, convincing—the
second even terrible in its reflections on how these days the holiest
madness is "understood" and cured. But their terror and irony alike
remain a little abstract—fading into illustrations of propositions out
of Riesman, or pressed hard toward some not-quite-committed religious position. I should suppose that if Roth is to be as funny and

as terrifying as he has the skill and insight to be, he must move out in the religious direction he has so far only indicated; but at the very least he must learn to risk a certain slovenliness, which in his short stories he evades with the nervousness of a compulsive house-cleaner. Other readers, I know, are more capable than I of responding to his pace, vigor and candor without the nagging sense that they are all a little compromised by something uncomfortably close to slickness; but I cannot deny that feeling in myself.

"Goodbye, Columbus" appeals to me, therefore, precisely because it is untidier than the rest, not so soon or so certainly in *control*. And in its generous margin of inadvertence, there is room enough for a mythical Newark, truth enough for the real one. In the end, "Goodbye, Columbus" does not quite work as a novella. Its plot (satisfactorily outrageous, but a little gimmicky and eked out with echoes of Mary McCarthy) and its themes tend to fall apart. Unlike some of the short stories, it evades rather than sub-mits to these themes, perhaps because the author is afraid to submit to the old-fashioned motif of love across class lines which struggles to become its point. But love, desperate and foredoomed, love as a betrayal which takes itself for pleasure, is the only subject adequate to the city Roth has imagined. This he knows really, and *inciden-tally* has exploited fully even in "Goodbye, Columbus."

It is in its incidents rather than in its total structure that the novella comes alive. Its details are as vivid as its themes are inert, its properties more alive, perhaps, than its chief protagonists: the furniture which symbolizes status, refrigerators crammed absurdly with mountains of fruit, a jockstrap hung from the faucet of a bath-tub, the record that gives the story its name. *Things* writhe, assert themselves, determine lives in a Dickensian frenzy. But some of the people who are possessed by them or subsist in the margins they leave free come alive, too—like Uncle Leo with his memories of the "oral love" which he learned from a girl called Hannah Schrei-ber at a B'nai Brith dance for servicemen, and which he exacted later from his wife, who was "up to here with Mogen David" after a Seder. "In fact, *twice* after Seders. Aachh! Everything good in my life I can count on my fingers." Here it seems to me is the pro-foundly atrocious pathos which is Roth's forte, his essential theme. Love in Newark! Beside it, the reminiscences of childhood, the anec-dotes of peacetime army life, even the accounts of the disruption of the Jew's suburban truce with respectability come to seem of secondary importance—preludes to a main theme.

Even as the legendary city which Roth creates is one looked back to at its moment of dying, so is the love which is proper to it. In his fables, the young watch with horror and without sympathy the old yearning desperately for an idyll of sex, whose unreality the decay of their own flesh declares; or the old, sleepless, hear from their beds the zip-zip of the young making out on the downstairs couch. The latter is the subject of "Epstein," for me the most successful of the shorter pieces despite a last-minute concession to sentimentality as banal as the required ending of a box-office movie. Urged by spring, the copulation of the young and the imminent failure of his own flesh, Epstein reaches out for romance with, naturally, the lady across the street. But he moves toward love through the drab horror of Newark whose embodiment he is, sagging, frantic, rather dreaming lust than enduring it; and he ends, as he must, convinced that he has syphilis, facing the prospect of a divorce, overtaken by a heart attack in the very act of love. " . . . his eyes were closed, his skin grayer than his hair. . . . His tongue hung over his teeth like a dead snake." And his wife looms over him with the proper advice, "You hear the doctor, Lou. All you got to do is live a normal life." It should be the end, but Roth gives it away—concludes with a promise of recovery and reconciliation. "You can clean it up? 'So it'll never come back,' the doctor said. . . ."

But maybe even this is all right. Maybe it is better because more terrible to imagine Epstein living than dead: he and his Goldie on their beach-chairs, with their Mounds bars, "in the cindery darkness of their alley"—while their nephew speeds toward a failure as complete as Epstein's, though his dream of love has been transformed from the lady across the street to the girl in Briarpath Hills.

Newark! A Florence it will never be in the minds of men, nor a Baghdad nor a Paris; but after Roth, we can hope that perhaps it will survive on library shelves ravaged by ambitious boys as another Yonville or Winesburg, Ohio—another remembered name for the "cindery darkness" which men build around themselves and in whose midst they suffer the indignities of love.

—1959

EIGHT

Antic Mailer–Portrait of a Middle-Aged Artist

SURELY THE MOST moving, truest, and saddest book to have appeared in the United States during the last year is Norman Mailer's *Advertisements for Myself*. It is a confession in the form of an anthology, an autobiography disguised as a running commentary on a chronologically arranged collection of Mailer's shorter writings over the past 20 years. There is a little of everything: short stories, newspaper columns, editorials, pseudo-poems, dramatic fragments. There are even selections from Mailer's already published novels (which he assumes, correctly, to have remained unread) and from one which he will clearly never finish.

There is the sense everywhere of a writer, baffled and near despair, trying for one last time to break through to the talent he dreamed he had at 17, to the audience he will not yet admit does not exist. Finally, and despite its occasional outbursts of apocalyptic hope, its praise of the Good Orgasm and the Hip Life, *Advertisements for Myself* is the story of the defeat of the writer in America—a work like, say, Griswold's *Life of Poe* or Edmund Wilson's recension of Scott Fitzgerald's *The Crackup*. Mailer, however, is his own Griswold and Wilson, denigrating critic and adulatory surviving friend all in one; and where he cannot himself provide sufficient occasion for self-hatred or self-pity, he draws on unfriendly reviews, nasty letters to the editor and accounts of private snubs.

"The shits are killing us," he tells us is the motto of his book; and there is evidence enough that he at least has been deeply

124

wounded by the shits in whose world American writers now, as in the time of Poe or Fitzgerald, have to fight for survival. It is the failure of others, of the "squares," that Mailer chiefly describes: the timidity of publishers, the venality or condescension of popular and academic reviewers, the vulgar spite of the purveyors of popular culture. But he betrays also the inadequacy of the hip world he considers his own: its ignorance and insularity, its hysterical pursuit of sensation, its small rivalries and paranoid fantasies. Mailer himself appears to believe that a radio interviewer deliberately doctored a tape to make Mailer's voice sound thin and fruity, his own voice rich and assured. What else can he believe, being convinced that he somehow just missed sparking the Coming Sexual Revolution in the columns of a small-circulation newspaper run by a friend, that it is the fear of his hipster's code of marijuana, jazz, and the orgasm which has made the publication of his books so difficult?

Yet the case Mailer makes against our culture is strengthened rather than weakened by the provinciality and paranoia which cue his accusations. That his frantic dedication to honesty and the unmitigated ambition which has driven him all his life should eventuate in a case history rather than in triumph, this is the final terror, a guilt in which we are all involved. What is there to choose, we are compelled to ask, between resisting the values of our society and acceding to them, if one means writing, like Mailer, inchoate and sentimental articles in *Dissent (e.g.,* "The White Negro"), and the other means composing dull appeals for cleaner television, like the article by Arthur Schlesinger Jr. in a recent *TV Guide?*

If there *were* a choice, I would, of course, stand with Mailer, whose enemies at least seem more like my own. But I cannot finally believe there is more than an illusion of choice; for I am haunted by a remembered scene, in which Schlesinger and an editor of *Dissent* are lounging at opposite ends of a fashionable Cape Cod beach and one cannot be sure to which party the Negro maid is hurrying with umbrella and baby bottle. Dying we surely are, but in a style to which it is hard to get accustomed!

As a matter of fact, it is precisely at the seaside in Wellfleet— and in the advertising offices among bright young sociologists, sure that they should be spending their time on something loftier than praising Coca-Cola—that a Mailer revival is now going on. "The conscience literature of the new $30,000-a-year men," one more than ordinarily self-conscious $30,000-a-year man recently called Mailer's novels; and it is this new popularity which Mailer has *not* come to terms with in the present book. It is a final irony before which even he flinches that he—who began as a middlebrow best-seller, then lapsed into obscurity—returns to popularity among a minority who find in his simple-minded intransigence on the subject of sex a metapolitics compatible with their own loss of youth and poverty. Such readers turn to Mailer not as a good writer, but as a rebel whose rebellion threatens (alas) nothing.

Indeed, Mailer is not a really first-rate novelist at all—and it is here that the pathos of his exemplary position is compounded. *The Naked and the Dead* is a cliché-ridden rewrite of the standard post-World War I protest novel, its villain-general half *Daily Worker* Fascist and half G.I. faggot. One is not surprised to learn in this volume that the book had been half-conceived by the under-graduate Mailer before he had ever left Harvard to go to the war. *Barbary Shore* is a belated thirties novel dissolved into incoherence by a hysteria irrelevant to its politics. And *The Deer Park,* for all its evident honesty, loses its sexual point amid the stereotypes of two decades of anti-Hollywood attitudinizing. Only now is Mailer beginning to escape from the limitations of the middlebrow protest novel, as he takes up—late as usual—the cause of the hipster and Reichian genitality.

Perhaps the best thing he has ever written is the outrageous and hilarious account (blow by blow and smell by smell) of a fore-doomed sexual encounter between a culturally pretentious coed (in analysis) and a sexual athlete, whose vanity and obtuseness one hopes Mailer perceives. Called in this collection "The Time of Her Time," the story will presumably be part of an immense novel, whose introduction, incredibly vacuous, concludes this book; and its protagonist is that same Sergius O'Shaugnessy who appeared in *The Deer Park*. Sergius was first imagined, we learn in these pages, as a mythically potent hero dreamed by "a small, frustrated man, a minor artist *manqué*." But he has unfortunately come to seem real to Mailer—not the embodiment of nostalgia for the unimaginable perfect orgasm but that orgasm made flesh. Without his counterfoil outside the dream he is the least credible male in modern fiction.

In *Advertisements,* however, the dreamer excluded from Mailer's fiction returns under the name of Norman Mailer, a real Hero of Our Time, the artist *manqué* unnerved alike by success and failure, reminded by his wife of how continually he goofs, endlessly en gaged in persuading himself that he is tough, although he can never forget he had to learn to fight from books. The Harvard Boy as Hipster and ex-Celebrated Author, he is put down by everyone: writers of letters to the papers, homosexual editors, TV interviewers —and not least of all by his amused, agonized, critical self.

Almost tenderly he anthologizes the insults of minor enemies and the rebuffs of those from whom most of all he wanted love— even the two writers whose child he feels himself, Hemingway and Faulkner. Tremulously, he sent *The Deer Park* to Hemingway, with an inscription asking for a reaction and with a proud, foolish warning that "if you do not answer . . . I will never attempt to communicate with you again." The package to which he entrusted book and love letter came back marked: "Address Unknown—Return to Sender."

With Faulkner, it was a little different, though the final result was not dissimilar. Not Mailer but an alert editor sent to the older writer Mailer's comment that "the white man fears the sexual potency of the Negro." Faulkner responded to this not-very-useful cliché that he had often heard the idea expressed "though not before by a man. The others were ladies . . . usually around 40 to 45 years of age." It was a stand-off: Mailer, who had over the air called Eisenhower a "woman," had been answered in kind, but he could not resist a last retort. His embarrassingly jejune answer does not matter: what counts is the fact that in painful candor he reports it with the rest of the interchange—completing to the final pathetic detail the Portrait of the Artist as a Middle-Aged Man, in which a generation can see itself and squirm: the unfulfilled writer, contemptuous of his peers, rebuffed by the mass audience, read by slobs and snubbed by the few elders he admires. Only a fool would confess to recognizing himself in such an image; but Mailer has had the final intelligence—or grace—to play for the world that torments him precisely such a fool—almost, indeed, the Fool.

—1960

NINE

Marx and Momma

IT BECOMES clearer and clearer these days that one of the chief functions of the sixties is somehow to rediscover, re-invent, redeem the thirties which, for the two decades before our own, seemed at a maximum distance from us—remote, unavailable. But the thirties were, of course, the period in which Jews were becoming, for the first time, spokesmen for America, or at least for that sentimental radicalism which best reflected the Depression mood of the United States. Michael Gold's *Jews Without Money* embodied that mood in fiction and Clifford Odets' *Waiting for Lefty* and *Awake and Sing* gave it form on the stage, both exploiting the rhythms of Jewish-American speech and the patterns of the Jewish-American family. What a strange marriage we celebrated then, without quite knowing it, between Karl Marx and the Jewish Mother.

But we can begin to know it now—in an age when everyone has read Henry Roth's *Call It Sleep* and Ph.D. candidates begin to write theses on Nathanael West; an age in which we are ready for Alfred Kazin's reminiscences of that decade and the confrontation most characteristic of it, between what he calls the "typical writers of the Twenties . . . rebels from 'good' families—Dos Passos, Hemingway, Fitzgerald, Cummings, Wilson, Cowley" and the "writers of the Thirties . . . from the working class, the lower class, the immigrant class . . . ," often enough, though not exclusively, the encounter of certain WASPS about to be driven from their positions of power and young Jews, like Kazin, about to make it in America on, to be sure, the highest cultural level.

Kazin's *Starting Out in the Thirties* is not entirely satisfactory as a unified work, moving erratically between personal reminiscence, capsule literary criticism and social history, but it is a fascinating record, a reminder of how radical politics and *avant-garde* book-reviewing became for the first time in the thirties a method of social climbing, especially viable for young Jews; and of how consequently, our own age of professors and pundits was in fact born.

But Kazin's book aspires to be more than a social record, indeed works best when it comes close to passing over into fiction —in the family scenes, for instance, dealing with his Cousin Sophie, which remind us of his more generally successful first book of reminiscences, *A Walk in the City.* I felt all through the book's scant length a tension between the logic of the material, which aspired to become a novel, and the caution of the writer, not finally trusting his own talent, or not able somehow to attain total honesty in regard to certain personal events that contain the book's truest meanings. The prose itself passes from delicacy and passion to a kind of virtuous woodenness every time the author withdraws from what is most dark, difficult and personal and commits himself to mere literary comment.

Nonetheless, if one is looking for a sense of what it was like to be alive and reading, ambitious, and literate in the thirties, Kazin's little book is an admirable guide. But how much pathos there is in the lapsed reputations of writers like Farrell and Saroyan, whose failed fame Kazin memorializes, or the evocation of an era in which it was possible to think Ralph Bates a great writer, and books like Malraux's *Man's Fate* or Silone's *Fontamara* masterpieces. From the vantage point of the sixties, one remembers that while Silone was being celebrated, the first translations of Alberto Moravia were going absolutely unnoticed in the United States, and relishes the dramatic irony of a note in Kazin's account of a meeting with James T. Farrell about a "young man comfortably draped on the couch" in Farrell's apartment who turned out to be Nathanael West.

A book Kazin does not at all mention, though it appeared in English in 1933 under the title of *The Sinner* and had stirred considerable popular response, is I. J. Singer's *Yoshe Kalb,* just now reissued under its original name and with an introduction by Singer's younger brother, Isaac Bashevis Singer, that darling of the sixties. In the few months since its publication, *Yoshe Kalb* appears to have stirred little or no enthusiasm, though it seems to me on re-reading even more moving and honest than I had remembered it—containing among other things one of the most magnificent portraits of an old country Jewish Bovary that I know.

We live, however, at a moment uncongenial to I. J. Singer's icy and uncompromising rationalism, his impatience with the world of *yiddishkeit* (he strove desperately for a while to find another language to write in) and especially with *chasidism,* about which we have learned—via Buber among others—to be sentimental and nostalgic. There is something ironical about the older Singer returning to us under the auspices of the younger, whose belief in demons we find so much more compatible with our own life than his brother's belief in reason. Nonetheless, *Yoshe Kalb* remains a rich and terrifying book, a vision of a world in decadence, ridden by corrupt and semiliterate rabbis, plagued by its own repressed lusts, but somehow redeemed by its longing to mythologize its experience in a way with which I. J. Singer found it harder than we do to sympathize—yet managed to all the same.

But this year sees the attempted revival of another thirties Jewish writer, also absent from the pages of Kazin's book; for just as he scants I. J. Singer in favor, say, of Malraux, so also he ignores Meyer Levin in favor of Edward Dahlberg, Albert Halper, Henry Roth, Daniel Fuchs, not to mention *goyim* like Henry Miller and Nelson Algren. Yet with the publication of *The Stronghold,* an attempt both historical and allegorical to come to terms with the Nazi experience, and Levin's fifteenth published book, his publishers have launched a campaign to get for him the critical acclaim they obviously (and he, too, of course must concur) feel his due. A pamphlet called "Meyer Levin at 60" lays out the history of his career and cites some of the praise he has been accorded from sources as various as Albert Einstein and Nelson Algren.

Moved by all this, I have been rereading him—not, to be sure, all of his books, which is a task beyond the scope of weak mortality, but much here and there; and once again, I rise from his work baffled. His books are not egregiously false; not embarrassingly inept; they deal with important subjects without unduly trivializing them; they are, in fact (after the false start of his first two novels, *Reporter* and *Frankie and Johnnie),* a continuing valiant effort to close with the meanings of being Jewish in an era which begins with the Leopold and Loeb Case and reaches a double climax with the defeat of Hitler and the emergence of the State of Israel. And if honesty and energy were enough, Levin would be—as he is not, alas—a writer of the first rank.

There is perhaps an unseemly hunger for violence in Levin, reflected in his sympathy with the Stern Gang and his obsession with Leopold and Loeb (though the book I admire most of all he has written is the fictional account of those two premature hipsters, *Compulsion*); and certainly there is a desire for establishing a version of heroism most critical readers find a little dismaying in an age when the antihero, the *shlemiel* as invented by Nathanael West and perfected by a host of latter-day imitators, seems more suitable to the meanings of our time. But it is finally a failure of language, an inability to rise above flatness to anything but vehemence and shrillness that keeps his work from kindling the imagination. *The Old Bunch*, published in 1937, remains still his major bid, his most substantial creation, but compared even to Farrell's *Studs Lonigan* trilogy (a book whose evaluation has continued to sag), it seems unforgivably dull, pulled by the banality of the world it imagines and should redeem into a corresponding banality.

Theater

There is some nostalgia for the thirties in the theater, too. Herbert Blau, for instance, insisting that the kind of moment he would like to recover for his Repertory Theatre at Lincoln Center is the one at the end of the original production of *Waiting for Lefty*, when the whole audience arose and yelled with the players "Strike!" Chiefly, however, the theater seems to clutch desperately at contemporaneity, the issue of the moment: which is, to be sure, race relations, or more specifically, *The Negro and the Jew*. This *chic* topic Howard Da Silva and company have introduced into the stage version of Dan Jacobson's *The Zulu and the Zayda*—Jacobson spelled it "zeide," but the change of spelling is the least among the degrading transformations of his material the vulgar and stupid play of almost the same name has achieved.

I should begin in all fairness by saying that the performance of Menasha Skulnick as the "zayda" or "zeide," as the case may be, is —though occasionally too cute—on the whole absolutely charming; and if the play could have been redeemed, he would have done so. But even his professional magic palls after what seems like hour upon hour of saying the most utterly banal things possible in *yiddish* (the very sound of which appears to break up the nostalgic audience), and then painfully translating them into English for the benefit of the *goyim*, if any, present. Only a mind childish enough to find inexhaustible fun in a large black African speaking our *mammeloshen* should subject himself to the play; though there is, to be sure, much pious material about race relations inserted between jokes, complete with explanatory sermons. The point of the whole self-righteous parable seems to be that all problems of *apartheid* in South Africa could be resolved if only a kindly old grandfather from the *shtetl* could confront a noble-hearted Zulu out of the *kraal,* and the two could trip through the streets of Johannesburg holding hands like young lovers.

Anybody interested in the original story, however, in which the Zulu wears a beard, the grandfather, who is not kindly, pees in bed, and there are no painfully explicit reflections on race relations, can find it in a recent collection called *Modern Jewish Stories* and edited by Gerda Charles. It is an oddly assorted anthology, containing things as bad as the unspeakable Hyman Kaplan stories of Leo Rosten and the hopelessly sentimental parable of Irwin Shaw, "Act of Faith"; but the original Jacobson study of a struggle between father and son that ends in virtual patricide is there, plus the not easily available story "The Hand that Fed Me," by Isaac Rosenfeld, whose fiction we are likely—to our loss—to forget exists.

Films

Oddly enough, race relations provide the main theme for the recent Israeli film *Sallah,* too. As a matter of fact, all that is most ticklish and difficult in Israeli life is touched on in this marvelously courageous movie, which, however, finks out at the very end with a conventional and unconvincing happy ending: the Israelis' contempt for the American Jews who subsidize them, the frittering away of the ideal of the *kibbutz* in endless ideological wrangling and the hiring of *Schwarzers* (well, black Jews anyhow) to do the hard labor, the permanence of "temporary housing," etc., etc.

I had expected nothing from the film, since the first Israeli movie I had ever seen—an incredible horse opera with the Israeli-cowboys beating out the Arab-Redskins—was so bad that I had decided Jewish moviemakers somehow mysteriously lost their skills in Israel. But *Sallah* turned out to be fast-moving, well-photographed, truly witty and marvelously acted, especially by Haym Topol who plays the title role. This film, too, has its share of jokes based on the use of Yiddish, but how different they are—the leader of a kibbutz for instance, whose Hebrew is ponderous and full of the loftiest abstractions, slipping into the *mammeloshen* when he counts out money. A little cruel to the tradition of *yiddishkeit,* perhaps, but no crueller than to American tourists, Israeli politicians, graft, fixed elections, and rigid bureaucracies in general.

Only Sallah himself emerges as a fully lovable figure, a kind of Oriental Jewish Old Black Joe, shiftless and conniving, noble-hearted and incorrigibly lazy by nature, earning a living by no work other than taking his Ashkenazi neighbor at backgammon day after day; but a criticism in his essence of the striving and progressive world into which the ingathering has plunged him. Of course, the writer of comedy can have it both ways; and so Ephraim Kishon, author of the script, does here, finally accepting the world his irony undercuts, and resolving his own contradictions by marrying off the children of the Black Jew, Sallah, to proper "white" *kibbutzniks.* It is an ending as easy and false in its way as that Howard Da Silva provides for the racial struggle in South Africa; but, after all, it is not the function of popular entertainers to solve the problems of ethnic conflict in Israel or the United States or Africa, only to charm us into believing in the darkness of the theater that we can dream them away. From this deluding dream great fiction and poetry must awaken us—and for this, too, we wait.

—1966

Some Jewish Pop Art Heroes

It was in 1913 that little Mary Phagan was killed, a thirteen-year-old factory girl, her attempted rape fumbled but her head successfully bashed in, and though it seems painfully clear now that her assailant was a Negro, her boss, a young Jew called Leo Frank, was convicted in court of her murder and lynched for it shortly thereafter. That was 1915, the war already begun which was to cut us off forever from that time of relative innocence; and Americans were going in large numbers to see *The Birth of a Nation,* greatest of all American moving pictures and storehouse of all the most vicious anti-Negro stereotypes. But just those Georgia rednecks, who should have contented themselves with an orgy of hating niggers and cheering the Ku Klux Klan under the auspices of D. W. Griffith, were letting the shiftless and violent Negro whose testimony doomed Frank slip through their fingers in order to indulge stereotypes more deeply buried in the depths of their psyches than any fantasies about Black sexuality. Harry Golden tells us that only a couple of decades ago, back-country performers were still singing the ballad he prints as an appendix to his best-selling book on the Frank Case *(A Little Girl Is Dead),* a ballad which justifies the lynching as sacred revenge against the Jews.

> Leo Frank he met her
> > With a brutish heart and grin;
> He says to little Mary,
> > "You'll never see home again."
> Judge Roan he passed the sentence;
> > He passed it very well;

The Christian doers of heaven
Sent Leo Frank to hell . . .

But why, Harry Golden is worrying all these years later, did the crowd malice of the Deep South, egged on by the rhetoric of Tom Watson, a splendid Populist leader gone sour and turned into nigger-baiter *par excellence,* why did it prefer the Jew to the Negro, given a clear choice? True enough, Frank behaved oddly in his first encounters with the police, appeared guilty of something (though God knows what), evasive, shifty; and by all accounts he seems to have been a singularly unappealing young man. Besides, he was clearly identified as a "capitalist," doubly a capitalist, since to the *lumpen* Socialist mind of the American Populist capitalist equals Jew, and the two together add up to demidevil. And in certain regards, the record seems to bear them out; for Frank did hire child labor, did work it disgracefully long hours at pitifully low wages; and if he did not (as popular fancy imagined) exploit his girls sexually, he walked in on their privacy with utter contempt for their dignity. Like most factory managers of his time, he was—metaphorically at least—screwing little girls like Mary Phagan; and in the undermind of the uneducated the line between metaphor and fact is blurred.

Besides, the kind of Georgians who lynched Frank were the inheritors of a folk tradition in which the Jew had been defined through centuries of song and story as the child-murderer. That tradition had been strong enough to influence great poets like Chaucer and Shakespeare and to create a score of ballads still sung in the rural South, so why should it not have moved the jurors, even before Frank's own lawyer had made the mistake of raising the issue of his Jewishness, and erupted finally in the fury of the lynch mob?

In European folk art, the Jew is a villain of a special kind, and before World War I the mind of back-country America was still folk and European; but in American Pop Art (which he plays a decisive role in creating) the Jew is a hero, like Golden himself: successful pop artist and pop idol—to the Gentiles, of course, as well as the Jews—at the same time. No wonder Norman Mailer, fighting the hard fight of the serious writer, who bucks rather than embodies the stereotypes of the mass audience, wrote plaintively once:

"If/Harry Golden/is the Gentile's Jew/can I be-/come the Golden/Goy?" This shift of the Jew from archetypal "Baddie" to mythological "Goodie," and its connection with the shift from folk culture to mass culture is immensely important yet almost totally ignored by literary critics like Irving Malin (in *Jews and Americans,* Southern Illinois University Press), who is committed to defining the nature of the Jewish experience in the United States.

Yet Malin does not mention Harry Golden, for instance, much less other Jewish Pop Art Heroes like Lenny Bruce, Sammy Davis, Jr., Jack Ruby, or Superman. Trying to fit Philip Roth and six other writers (Bellow, Malamud, Karl Shapiro, etc.) into his own seven categories (Exile, Time, Irony, Parable, etc.), he does not find an occasion for treating the difficult and essential subject I have been trying to define. Perhaps this is because "vulgarity" is not one of his rubrics, and it is the vivid and perdurable vulgarity of the Jews (so embarrassing to our official apologists) which lies at the heart of Pop Culture. No Jew on his own would have invented —thank God—the notion of a gentleman, but some Jews invented Miami Beach, some the commercial Musical Comedy, and two, Jerome Siegel and Joe Shuster, the Comic Book—or at least, the first Great Comic Book Hero of them all, Superman.

We live now at a point where the generation (they must be somewhere between twenty-five and thirty-five) that grew up on the classic Comic Book is memorializing it; making a smash success out of the revived Bat Man on TV (pop art wryly remembered is Camp, a kind of genteel tribute to vulgarity); and, I hope, buying in vast quantities the annotated anthology of the genre recently put together by Jules Feiffer, himself a veteran vulgarian *(The Great Comic Book Heroes).*

Jules Feiffer loves the comic books a little better than he understands them, missing, I think, the essential point that they are a special kind of "junk" in the history of subart: *urban junk*—their imagined world simply the city, and their heroes city boys or losers in the very world that makes and peddles the comics (Superman is in "real life" an unsuccessful reporter). But the dreamers in the city are, almost inevitably, Jews—and it is their fantasies by which a generation or two lived, their fantasies by which they discovered they could make it in this Gentile world: beginning in school, let's say, by drawing the pictures erotic or heroic, which their inept neighbors needed to see before they were quite sure what they were dreaming.

Not only Will Eisner's seedy *The Spirit* was Jewish, as Feiffer sees; but all of those more WASPish looking Superfellows, though on another level. They are Jewish versions of the Goy, idealized portraits of the Gentile boy who beats up the Jewish one (no wonder so many of their fictional victims had long noses and puttered about laboratories)—quite like, on their level, Bellow's Henderson or Mailer's Sergius O'Shaughnessy. Did we love them or hate them, those dumb sluggers in their lodge regalia? The answer is there in the record as Feiffer sees quite clearly when dealing with their female opposite numbers, who remind us of that other perfect bully out of the nightmares of our childhood: Mama. ". . . Wonder Woman . . . was every Jewish boy's unfantasied picture of the world as it really was. You mean men were not wicked and weak? . . . You mean women didn't have to be *stronger* than men to survive in this world? Not in *my* house?"

Once he has projected his oppressor as his secret self, however, the Jewish writer, on a pop level or any other, is likely to get in trouble; end like Norman Mailer—or Lenny Bruce—forgetting that he is only Jerome Siegel imagining he is Clark Kent dreaming that he can reveal himself as Superman, and coming to believe that there is only himself, i.e., Super-Jew. Lenny Bruce's autobiography *(How to Talk Dirty and Influence People)* does not take us to the point where he recently fell out of a hotel window, after having capered madly about the room and lifted an imaginary cape, screaming, "I'm Super-Jew." But it does take us through some of his earlier disguises as an Oriental mystic, Roman Catholic priest, transvestite sailor, still uncertain of his destiny as victim, persecuted truth-teller, gross and grotesque prophet—his passion called obscenity, and his madness drug addiction. There is a streak of self-dramatizing sentimentality in Lenny Bruce that tempts him to see himself as Jesus Christ; but there is a saving vulgarity, too, which impels him to realize that he is rather a Comic Book Hero who cannot fly. That vulgarity I'm sure he would be pleased to think of as Jewish; for he is (with scarcely any Jewish education or even background, certainly none of the kind generally called "positive") much concerned with sorting out the world into what he thinks of as its primary categories: "Evaporated milk is goyish even if the Jews invented it. Chocolate is Jewish and fudge is goyish. Spam is goyish and rye bread is Jewish. Negroes are all Jews. Italians are all Jews. Irishmen who have rejected their religion are Jews. Mouths are very Jewish. And bosoms. Baton-twirling is very goyish." In his sense at least, it is still hard to be a Jew; and perhaps the chief value of his book (along with the thousand bitter laughs it provides) is to remind us of this fact.

No one would suspect it, on the other hand, reading Sammy Davis, Jr.'s autobiography; for though, like Lenny Bruce, he is an entertainer who has turned himself into a Pop Art Hero, he is one who has made it—in part, he would have us believe, by identifying with the Good Medicine of Judaism. Waking from a difficult and successful operation, he finds "a clear outline of the Star of David" impressed on his palm from a religious medallion he was clutching; he wears a mezuzah, given him by Eddie Cantor, around his neck and charms everyone; he gains the respect of Sam Goldwyn by refusing to work on Yom Kippur; he wins a beautiful *shiksa* for his wife, who then converts to Judaism and their wedding is a B. O. smash! Yet all through it of course, he is a Negro. Under such circumstances, who wouldn't be a Jew!

His book *(Yes I Can),* though professionally written in that insipid ghost style which robs truth of conviction and fact of reality, is not without interest. For somehow the picture of a vain, driven, essentially unlovable man, at odds with his own Negro community (and what disheartening glimpses we have of their columnists, reporters, and millionaires) and himself, emerges, a gifted entertainer who betrays almost everything and everybody but is blessed with success; and who—in this age of strange conversions—imagines that to begin to become "all right," one must become a Jew. I saw, for my sins, the production of *Golden Boy* just now closing in New York, an utterly incredible revision of Odets' soupy play about Jews updated to get the box office that only Negro drama gets these days; and in the midst of it all Sammy Davis, trying to live the part he acted, a Negro turned Jew being the John Garfield of the sixties. And remembering, of course, Marilyn Monroe and Elizabeth Taylor, I found myself slipping away into a daydream in which Frank Sinatra (second only unto Jehovah in Sammy Davis' pantheon) would end up playing Frankie Alpine in the movie made of Bernard Malamud's *The Assistant,* and insisting upon being really circumcized in the last scene where that character becomes a Jew. And then there would be no goyim left at all in the world of pop culture, not a single one. . . .

But walking down the street afterward, I saw the lines queued up before *Thunderball* and realized that James Bond at least was left, the last of the WASP heroes, as goyish as fudge or twirler girls: something for us to imagine ourselves when we grew weary of the mythic burden of our Jewishness. My relief did not last long, however; for just as there is (in the local drugstore, supermarket, airport newsstand) a Fanny Hillman of our own these days for every one of *their* Fanny Hills, I discovered there is also an Israel Bond, OY-OY-7, the sort-of hero of *Loxfinger,* which surely must rank with the worst books ever written. I will not let chauvinism drive me to calling it unequivocally *the* worst; but if you have wondered where all the weary Semitic jokes went since Hitler scared them out of the goyim they are here (along with Hitler himself), in such a context of Borsht Belt good humor that one must take them as innocently proffered. Next to Sol Weinstein, author of *Loxfinger,* Henny Youngman seems like Oscar Wilde; and it takes a considerable effort to remember the immemorial principle that, despite everything, a Jew has a right to make a living.

Vulgarity passes over into grossness not by excess but by cold-blooded commercial manipulation. What could be more vulgar, for instance, yet still pathetic at least, perhaps even tragic, than Jack Ruby who wanted, like any kid reading *Superman,* to be a hero, too; and even got the chance to do it on television. John Kaplan and Jon R. Waltz have written their recent study of the case *(The Trial of Jack Ruby)* to analyze courtroom strategies, not the vagaries of mass culture; but it is the latter that impressed and disheartened me as I made my way through their book: NBC offering to pick up the tab if Ruby would hire the real-life original of TV's *Sam Benedict;* Judge Brown's public denial of the manuscript about the case by which he hoped to make his fortune; Ruby's lawyers bootlegging pictures of him to sell to *Life,* etc., etc.

In his own deepest consciousness, however, Ruby wanted to sell nothing, only to show the world (on television if possible) that "Jews do have guts," that under his own improbable guise Super-

Jew really lived and would avenge the President that had been kind
to his people. Once convicted and, he felt, vilified, however, it was
quite other fantasies that possessed Ruby's poor paranoid head:
fantasies that "all the Jews in America were being slaughtered,"
"twenty-five million innocent people," and that even his brother
Sam was being "tortured, horribly mutilated, castrated and burned
in the street outside the jail"—that the Jew had, in fact, become
Leo Frank again because he had failed to be Superman.

But Ruby is, of course, wrong. No crowds are gathering for his
lynching or his brother's; and if any ballads are being made now,
they concern not his guilt but his plight, are sung not by rednecks
from the hills but urban folk singers, Jews like Bobby Dylan, the
inventors of "folk-rock," who surely celebrate him something like
this:

> I didn't raise my chubby, sweet,
>   brown-eyed balding boy
> To go out and overdo the doin's
>   of some goy.
> He murdered a man on TV
>   They say he has shot another.
> Won't you give some thought to
>   poor Jack Ruby's mother.

—1966

ELEVEN

This Year We Are Slaves—
Next Year We Shall Be Free

To say who the Jews are, to speculate about what the Jews will become (or, alternatively, what will become of the Jews), to remember what the Jews were—surely these have always been the obsessive tasks of those who by that very token we have continued to call
Jews. But when these preoccupations become the center of a novelist's concern, he is driven to attempt that most difficult of forms of
fiction, the historical novel; and it is precisely four historical novels,
four *Jewish* historical novels (plus a pair of Jewish historical films)
about which I have been pondering over the past couple of weeks.

The longest and most ambitious (and by all odds the worst) of
the lot is by a non-Jew, who, despite his detached position, seems to
have been as deeply troubled in his genteel, liberal soul as any genteel, liberal Jew by the two recent events which trouble all the writers with whom I am dealing—the atrocious fact of Hitler's rise and
fall on the one hand, and the ambiguous triumph of Israel on the
other. It is with Israel that James Michener is primarily concerned;
and in *The Source* he uses the device of an archeological dig to
take us back via a series of historical flashbacks some 100,000
years into the past of what used to be called the Holy Land. Even
as popular archeology, this book seems to me dull and thin—the
thickest thin book I have read. Mr. Michener sees the toughness
and courage of the Israelis all right, just as he sees their most difficult problems (discrimination against "Black Jews," tyranny of an
Orthodox rabbinate, etc., etc.), but somehow none of this hurts him

enough, ultimately concerned as he is with the pale, Protestant question: how can Judaism remain a valid religion after the appearance of the Christian Church.

Even Stephen Longstreet's *Pedlock and Sons,* for all its commitment to the weariest middlebrow banalities about the meaning of American life and all its obvious popular appeal (lots of outward action, old-fashioned heavy-handed plotting and explicit sex), says a little more about what it feels like to be conscious of one's self as a Jew than Mr. Michener's blandly righteous book. It is about the American scene, of course, that Mr. Longstreet writes, of how the Jews made it in America, and what they did when they got there. But even in his more modest attempt, he has trouble assimilating his gobbets of historical information. For me, the journal entries were an invitation to skipping I could not resist.

Dan Jacobson's attempt in *The Beginners* to do an analogous family saga of the Jews in South Africa is much more sober and serious, the work of a much more gifted writer, though I suspect his gifts qualify him for humor and gentle pathos rather than for the ambitious solemnities of this novel which is profoundly unexciting, technically unadventurous, unforgivably well behaved. Surely the emigration of Jews from the Pale to the New World of South Africa, from South Africa to England and Israel, much less their spiritual wanderings from Orthodoxy to Marxism and Zionism and back to Orthodoxy again cannot be that dull.

Mr. Bassani's *The Garden of the Finzi-Continis* is the slimmest and tightest of the books I have been reading—the most deceptively modest, and finally the most successful. A description of the last days of a Jewish community in a provincial Italian city, Bassani's book stays in the mind with a peculiar persistence. It creates not real Jews, perhaps, but the ghosts of real Jews—as unheroic, tentative and ridden by vanity as any of us, but no more deserving surely of being dead.

To resist the impulse toward the heroic in recalling the recent Jewish past requires a kind of quiet heroism which Bassani, in fact, possesses. Not so the authors (script writer, producer, director) of *Cast a Giant Shadow,* which attempts to memorialize the creation of the State of Israel in what moviemakers like to call "epic" terms

—and which has drafted for its purposes such prototypes of heroism on the screen as John Wayne and Kirk Douglas (the latter casting off at last his *goyish* camouflage and playing the Jewish "jock" he really is). In the end, what was hard enough to believe to begin with is made even more incredible. But perhaps it is the function of the "big movie" to make the truth seem false enough to bear.

How much better the antiheroic tact of *The Shop on Main Street* which plays out the immediate events of the destruction of Mid-European Jewry as if seen through the wrong end of a telescope, reduced in size but increased in intensity of focus. This extraordinary Czech film has just been awarded an Oscar, which seems to me even more extraordinary, since I, at least, expect the Academy Awards to go unerringly where they belong, to standard mediocrity of high technical excellence. But perhaps even in Hollywood there are ceremonial occasions when vice pays tribute to virtue.

Each of these works involves dreaming as well as remembering, evoking, side by side with its political memories, erotic dreams. In *The Source,* the contemporary plot is actually a parable in which a beautiful Israeli archeologist hesitates long over which of three contenders she shall marry: a fellow Israeli, a Catholic American or (a dark horse who enters at the last moment) a rich American Jew. And when this improbable Hebrew Astarte casts her lot with the last, leaves Israel for Chicago, and the pioneer life for suburbia, she expresses surely Michener's own final uneasiness with Israel and the female sexuality he deems appropriate to it.

Pedlock and Sons is sexier by far, possessed not by the author's dreams of a Gentile for whom the Jewish girl represents the forbidden sexual object, but the bolder fantasies of a Jew for whom the *shiksa* plays an analogous mythological role; and there are *shiksas* aplenty in its pages—red-haired secretaries, luscious Armenian spies, etc., etc. The best and most auspicious sex in the novel, however, turns out to involve two nice Jewish kids, leading them on to marriage (the girl protests loudly at one point that she is *not* Marjorie Morningstar, but she fools no one).

Dan Jacobson has a harder time being fashionably frank about sex; for despite the assurance of the book jacket that its world is one "of sexual explicitness and racial conflicts," it is really resolutely old-fashioned and muted by archaic reticences.

Perhaps the essential virtue of Bassani's book is that it allows its love story, its dream of love, to make its point without burying it beneath a ponderous superstructure of sociological or political observations.

As everyone knows, however, the real dream girl of the Jewish boy—whether he writes books or not—is his mother; and we are not surprised to find that in both Longstreet's and Jacobson's novels the Beloved who binds the fiction together in feeling and form is the Matriarch. In *Pedlock and Sons* she is, to be sure, more Wife of Bath than standard Jewish Mother; but in *The Beginners* she returns in her conventional form, one whose erotic longing, baffled in her husband, is invested ambiguously in her sons. And Jacobson, aware of her mythological dimensions, even calls her Sarah.

One of the two chief characters of *The Shop on Main Street* is a Jewish-Mother-without-a-son gone senile, who blindly takes in as her substitute son a poor goy, who in turn thinks of himself as exploiting her under cover of the anti-Semitic regulations of the Czech Nazi puppet government. He is, however, not very good at exploiting, this simple-minded peasant, though under pressure he turned out to be (like all of us) adequate enough at betrayal—thus acting out not only the role of the Bad Gentile Neighbor at the time of the Holocaust, but of the Bad Jewish Son at any time.

Indeed, I suspect that part of the enormous appeal of the movie may depend precisely on its stirring the guilt feelings planted in all of us by *our* mothers—along with its portrait of evil personified in the too-sexual wife of the protagonist, its appeal to the audience to cheer or at least grimly approve when at long last he beats the hell out of her. What could be more American, or Jewish for that matter, more Jewish-American, more universal at the moment, than simultaneously to hate the wife, love mama, and deplore the death of Europe's Jews. Maybe, after all, only an Academy Award can signify how terrifyingly near to all of our ugly hearts this beautifully rendered fable comes.

—1966

TWELVE

Myths of the Jews on
Stage and Screen

IT IS NOT easy to lie about what happened at Auschwitz now that the facts are known, but Peter Weiss in *The Investigation* has managed to do so—and for this he must be given, I suppose, some kind of credit though his method is simple and not original with him. He has merely removed from the story—the Jews. His carefully edited text, drawn from the records of a trial of Nazi war criminals held in Frankfurt between January 1964 and August 1965, omits the word "Jew" as if somehow it were irrelevant or, worse, misleading; as if the bulk of the four million victims destroyed there were Jews only by accident or mistake. I do not believe, as do some more charitable reviewers of his play, that he desires to universalize the terrible events which reached their climax in the gas chambers and ovens. Far from it; the Soviet Union is mentioned quite specifically over and over along with the names of certain large industrial concerns, so that finally we are left with the impression that what really happened to the six million under Hitler was only an incident in the class struggle, or more precisely the clash between German Big Business and the Communist Party. But rendered in light of this simple-minded Marxist interpretation of Nazism, what happened at Auschwitz seems trivialized, desecrated, profaned.

We need a myth of Hitlerism, all right, some large archetypal view in which all that is merely bureaucratic or narrowly political or simply sadistic in the appalling record will be raised to a level above journalism and pornography; but Party-line propaganda will not do. To be sure, one member of the small audience present on the night I attended the play was moved to rise in the balcony and scream: "The United States is doing exactly the same thing, using gas and killing children in Vietnam!" I presume, however, he had brought his politics with him and was merely taking advantage of the occasion to force those foolish enough to be present to endure yet one more small indignity. Never mind the feeble-minded politics, in any case, the obtuseness which made me almost ashamed for the moment of my own opposition to the War in Vietnam; what mattered much more was the gratuitous second destruction of German Jewry, the erasing from history of those history had already killed. And for this, Communist politics (with its own bad conscience about the Jews) is only partly to blame, since Peter Weiss is apparently the victim of a personal hang-up in this regard. I heard him last year, for instance, speaking at Princeton under the auspices of the *Gruppe '47,* deliver a long conversion speech, explaining how he had come to see the light about what was going on in Germany—in which also he did not ever use the word Jew; and I understood for the first time (began to understand, at least) why he pretended that his earlier play about Marx and Freud, which is to say, about a pair of ex-Jews, was actually a dialogue between two unexceptionable *goyim,* Marat and the Marquis de Sade. Peter Brook's splendid version of that first drama, the extraordinary passion and color of the production, had concealed from me Weiss's real limitations: his deficient sense of drama, his banality on the level of ideas, his sick fascination with horror, and his crippling fear of his own Jewishness. The latter two are surely part of the heritage of Hitlerism, telling an implicit truth about Weiss and his world, that on an explicit level he does not know how to confess. And though it perhaps does him more honor than he deserves, we must be willing to identify him as yet one more victim of the ultimate horror, the last flowering of European anti-Semitism which includes in its toll countless thousands of living Jews along with the six million dead.

Hitler is, as I recall, as absent from Weiss's pseudodrama as are the Jews themselves; for the archetypal destroyer baffles the mean secular mind of the journalist-propagandist as utterly as the victims themselves: those we must understand—whatever their personal inadequacies and failures in self-consciousness—to have been bearing witness, "Sanctifying," as some Jews are still able mythologically to say, "the Name." How much more moving, deeply terrifying, *true* is the appearance which Hitler makes in Leonard Cohen's recent novel, *Beautiful Losers* (it is a book which does not fade from my mind, which I find myself driven to recall and mention on all possible occasions), an obscene spirit evoked in the midst of a passage which presents itself as mere fiction, frank pornography—rather than at the heart of a lubricious lie which purports to be a "document." Two of his characters have yielded themselves up to an infinitely versatile exciter of the flesh, an omnipurpose sex machine called a "Danish Vibrator," which has made each of them "nothing but a buffet of juice, flesh, excrement, muscle to serve its appetite." And then:

> There was a professional knock on the blond door.—It must be him, I said.—Should we put our clothes on?—Why bother. We did not even have to open the door. The waiter had a pass-key. He was wearing the old raincoat and moustache, but underneath he was perfectly nude. We turned toward him. — Do you like Argentine? I asked for the sake of civil conversation.

And mysteriously, there is evoked not merely a shudder, but a sense of the obscenity of it all, the odd sexual repulsion-allure essential to the tale of the Camps. Though this time around not suffered in self-deception by author and audience, rather caught, exposed, brought out into the open. And I therefore felt reading it *clean,* as I do not coming on articles about the destruction of Jewry in the popular press, or hearing from Weiss's players the whole terrible bit about the nakedness of the victims in the gas chambers, the hardening cement introduced into the vaginas of Jewish women, etc., etc. The sheer *dirtiness* of the experience on the most literal level, the pornographic horror of the Camps is not, I know, incidental but essential—but this is hard to confront, much less to understand. Some light is cast on it, of course, by Weiss's favorite *bête noire,* the Marquis de Sade, but even more by the New Testament; for ultimately it is from that insidious compendium of myth that the whole notion of the "dirty Jew"—on which the anti-Semite's necessary sense of defilement depends—arises. Stripped to the buff and sent to "the showers": this is how Jews died at Auschwitz —those obdurate people who would not be washed clean in the Blood of the Lamb. "Let those who are filthy remain filthy," says one of the Gospels; and who are in this sense filthier than the killers of Christ?

We have long been the victims of an obscene myth of ourselves as the obscene enemies of man and God; and we must make the experience that revealed to victim and victimizer alike the depth of its obscenity a myth of equal stature and terror—lest its meanings be frittered away in the "historical record." But where are our mythologizers? Not Weiss certainly, who will not even grant that we exist mythologically. And if not even a German Jew steeped in the intimate horror of it all can make myth of the experience, what can we expect of remoter Americans?

Not very long ago I went finally, though a little reluctantly, to see Pasolini's extraordinarily deft and beautiful filming of that deep source of anti-Semitic mythology, *The Gospel According to Saint Matthew*. How beautiful the faces in it were, and the Italian countryside, and the costumes right out of Piero della Francesca; and how terrifying the fable, how satisfactorily villainous the High Priests and the fickle mob of Jews! For me as a Jew in attendance, it was an experience much like that of, say, an Indian kid on a reservation watching a cowboy and Indian film and barely resisting the impulse to cheer for the wrong side. "Remember you're an Indian, for Christ's sake," I found myself telling myself at one point; and I wanted to scream the same sentence aloud up into the screen, when I recognized there the talented Italian-Jewish novelist, Natalia Ginzburg, playing, of all things, the part of Martha: *Remember, you're an Indian, too.*

There is a fascinating little book which bears on this subject. Written by a priest called Edward H. Flannery and entitled *The Anguish of the Jews: Twenty-three Centuries of Anti-Semitism,* it is currently available in paperback, published by Macmillan, and is causing at the moment widespread controversy in the liberal Catholic press. Father Flannery tries, God knows, to break the long silence of the Church on this subject, but he cannot resist qualifying, justifying and apologizing when specifically Christian anti-Semitism (as opposed to anti-Semitism practiced by Christians despite their own religion) becomes the issue; finally falling back on earlier authority when the question of the anti-Semitism of the Gospels themselves is posed: "We conclude with Father Baum: There is no foundation for the accusation that a seed of contempt and hatred for the Jews can be found in the New Testament. . . ." But this most Jews find difficult to accept, subscribing—despite occasional temptations to claim Jesus as "one of our boys"—to the belief recently formulated once more by Hugh J. Schonfield in a book called *The Passover Plot:* "The calumny that the Jewish people were responsible for the death of Jesus has all along been an anti-Semitic fraud perpetuated by the Church. . . ." It is hard to take with full seriousness a man who insists on calling himself "Dr." on the jacket and title page of his book; and there is little in Schonfield's book (including the theory that Jesus was drugged and prepared for a fake resurrection, or that his enemies were the "aristocrats" among the Jews opposed to the "common people") which is new or startling. But there is one sentence for which it may be remembered beyond its merits (for which I, at any rate, will recall it with some pleasure), in which the author says of Jesus: "He had what is called in Jewish jargon a *yiddishe hertz,* a Jewish warmth of benevolent affection." Which is, one likes to think, an unacknowledged quotation from that Jewish mother whom misguided Christians insist on thinking of as the Blessed Virgin.

But, of course, Christians have long carried with them, not only the mythology of the New Testament so hostile to us, but our own self-justifying mythology as preserved in what they call The Old Testament—equally a part of their revered "Bible." And John Huston's recent *The Bible* turns out to be, for once, that first half of the Scriptures only, concluding with Abraham's deliverance from the obligation of human sacrifice, in short, *"our* Bible." But John Huston's film is finally, alas, a contribution neither to the well-being of the Jews nor to the art of cinema. It is fine in its first moments, which is to say, until humans and animals appear—spectacularly handsome in its evocation of the creation of the physical universe, of boiling seas and ragged rocks. But from then on it is a shambles: in casting (imagining a naked Eve, Huston naturally imagines a Swedish actress; and conceiving of the first Jews, perversely insists that Sarah our Mother is Ava Gardner and Father Abraham,

George C. Scott); in language (arranged and edited with supplementary revelation by Christopher Fry, the very words of Scripture become banal and flat); but especially in discretion and tact.

The scenes in the Garden of Eden are a kind of coy striptease, in which our naked first ancestors dodge from one conveniently masking bush or tree limb to another, concealing from all the fact that they have nipples or genitals—and revealing themselves at full length only from behind; so that finally we have the sense that the first man and first woman were two pairs of buttocks with nothing on the other side. The Noah's Ark sequence, on the other hand, is for the whole family—a Walt Disney movie in which kindly old Noah moves among animals so impossibly cute that a cynical viewer finds himself wishing they had not made it into the ark. John Huston has always been queer for elephants, but never so flagrantly sentimental about it all. Even so, he is less intolerable as Disney than as Cecil B. DeMille, into whose manner he is tempted by the Tower of Babel and the corruption of Sodom and Gomorrah. But nowhere does he seem fresh or vivid or true. What we are given is a reading of Genesis not as terrifying and primitive myth allegorized into something like wisdom, but as a child's or a fundamentalist backwood preacher's notion of history, passed via classic comic books or illustrated Sunday school texts to the screen. From time to time, Huston pretties up the traditional account to make God look good—perhaps because, like all makers of Biblical Epic Movies, he begins before he is through to think he is God. Perhaps it is too much to expect a sophisticated version of the legends upon which our deepest self-consciousness as Jews largely depends; this is not after all what we go to the movies to get. But at least a man of Huston's immense zest might have given us something as richly vulgar and riotous as, say, the Mystery Plays of the Middle Ages, in which Noah, far from being a benevolent patter of elephants' trunks, was a hoary old drunk harried by a loud-mouthed shrew. Ah well, even from so great a moviemaker as Huston, I suppose, we can expect triumphs of vulgarity only by mistake; and Billy Wilder himself I fear confronted by Scriptures would be overtaken by that solemn piety which has made so many Christians secret haters of their own dearest mythology—and therefore of the Jews who, they dimly surmise, had something to do with the beginnings of it all.

—1967

THIRTEEN

Crimes and Punishments

THERE IS AN odd sense these days in the still flourishing community of Jewish-American writers that a certain vein of material is nearing exhaustion, that the mother lode which it once seemed would last forever is at the point of being used up. How long, after all, is it possible to exploit a diminishing tradition of *yiddishkeit,* which becomes finally nothing more than a memory of that diminishing tradition, a tradition of the memory of the tradition, etc., etc., to the point of absolute zero. In the work of such ultimate Jews as Bruce Jay Friedman one has the feeling of a diminuendo in content made all the more terrifying by the mounting laughter it occasions. And the publication of Bellow's *Herzog* seems somehow to have smacked of finality—representing for all its versatility and skill the end of something rather than a beginning. I do not mean to say that *Herzog* may not be a book of first excellence (I do not find it so, but this may arise from some deficiency or weariness in me), merely that its net effect is dispiriting. *Herzog,* in any event, seems to move the middle-aged more than it does the young, and being myself middle-aged, Herzog-aged, to be quite frank, I find this especially dismaying.

It has been quite a while as such things go—in a period where literary generations succeed each other with terrifying rapidity—since there has been a youth best-seller by a Jewish American writer. The last was J. D. Salinger's *Catcher in the Rye,* and even in that case he had to pretend that young Holden was a *goy.* The last two books to have moved large numbers of the young with the sense of speaking from as well as to them have been Christian allegories: William Golding's *Lord of the Flies* and J. R. R. Tolkien's

Lord of the Rings. But these at least are properly Christian, which is to say, connected in some way with the basic mythology and the great themes of Judaism.

And of all this, at some level or other, Jewish American writers begin to grow aware. I do not think anyone is surprised that the boom in Jewishness has not continued indefinitely; some critics have been predicting for quite a while, I among them, that soon, soon the Negroes would be asserting their right to be spokesmen for America as a whole; and that it was not excluded that the White Anglo-Saxon Protestants might make a sort of posthumous bid for immortality. But no one, I think, had foreseen that the Jewish-American subject matter and diction and style might give out (or worse be institutionalized, become established) before the switch-over came. Who before, in the Western World, had imagined Establishment Jews! But the Negroes have been slow in taking over the spokesman role, and the WASPS somehow do not quite fill the bill; so that we are confronted with a generation of Jewish-American writers, more full of vigor than matter, in search of a new subject.

One at least has made the desperate attempt to renew himself by turning to the past, switching from the evocation of things lived through in his own generation to the re-creation of what happened just beyond the rim of his knowing, in history. Jewish historical novels have been written before, to be sure; but they have tended to come out of a remote, easily romanticized past, not like Bernard Malamud's *The Fixer,* out of a history just over the horizon, as close to us and as related to events that have made our world (consequent anti-Semitism, the Russian revolution) as the Beilis case which provided the documentary evidence of punishment without a crime that Malamud has tried to mythicize and generalize. In the end, however, what appeal his book has for me is not in style or tone, a pastiche of translated Russian and Yiddish books, but in the resonance of the actual case behind it—for which, after all, one might as well read Maurice Samuel's high-level journalistic account, *Blood Accusation.* I do not mean that there is not genuine pathos in Malamud—feeling on the verge but not over the edge of sentimentality is his forte—but that his book resolves nothing of the crisis in the Jewish-American novel in which I feel myself deeply involved. Finally, his book bores me, offends me with the sense that nothing is happening in it except history, old history. What is the point, I find a troubled voice in my head asking, in writing one more nineteenth-century novel past the middle of the twentieth century?

In retrospect, I think more and more that Malamud's best novel was his first one—that mythological study of baseball and the hatred of the Hero called *The Natural*. But he was trying an interesting tack at least in his unsuccessful last one, too, *A New Life,* in which he tried to portray the interior exile of an urban Jew in the American West, the Jew in an improbable, less-exploited locale than New York or Chicago or wherever. His West and his Jew kept coming apart, however, perhaps because of his deficient sense of the former; and so he ended not by writing a Western with a Jewish accent but only one more weary college novel.

David Markson, in a little noticed novel which appeared well over a year ago now, did much better, producing a broad burlesque of Indian and cowboy relations seen with a learned and irreverent eye. His *The Ballad of Dingus Magee* is full of bad jokes and good history, plus some of the best Indian stuff next to the Catherine Tekakwitha story in Leonard Cohen's *The Beautiful Losers* ever to have been produced out of the Jewish-American imagination, specially qualified on this score by detachment and ignorance—two great possible sources for the New Western. Other Jews have tried their hand at the revived Western genre, too—Arthur Miller, for instance, in both the original story and the later screenplay called *The Misfits;* and I myself in my last novel, *Back to China,* as well as the final story in my recent collection of fiction, *The Last Jew in America.*

That story, *The Last Spade in the West,* is, as the title declares, concerned also, in fact primarily, with the Negro; and here, perhaps, is the real chance for the Jewish-American writer bereft of a theme or left with one too long worked over. Not only have Negro writers of real distinction been slow to appear (Baldwin seems at a dead end; Ralph Ellison writes with painful slowness and in the tradition of Kafka; LeRoi Jones finds it hard to make art of an obsession which grows more and more painful until it verges on simple *mishigas),* but there has been developing between Negroes and Jews a kind of relationship which only literature can manage to express in all its involved agony—a relationship of mutual distrust and bafflement which makes all political or sociological wisdom seem inept platitude.

For the first time in modern memory the Jews find themselves not in the traditional position of the exploited, but in the uncomfortable new position of the exploiter—at least in the consciousness of Negroes, yelling to their faces and muttering behind their backs, "Down with Ikey Goldberg." The ironies of this situation no Negro writer has as yet developed on the level of art; but two new novels, *Big Man* by Jay Neugeboren and *Call the Keeper* by Nat Hentoff, developed reflections on the theme from the point of view of the Jewish writer ferociously identifying with the Negro. The Neugeboren book is the less rewarding of the two, content by and large with easy humor and obvious pathos, as it describes the plight of a Negro basketball player, blackballed after the game-fixing scandals in the Garden, and victimized—perhaps with the best of intentions —by a Jewish journalist on the make, who discovers him playing for a B'nai Brith championship in a Brooklyn synagogue. Hentoff, on the other hand, plunges us deep into the world of hipsterism, jazz, and dope, in the midst of which there is improbably re-enacted a new up-to-date version of Dostoevsky's *Crime and Punishment*, but this time American style, with a Negro psychopath in the Raskolnikov role and a Jewish detective as the malign pursuing cop.

And obviously it will not stop here, since the Jewish writer in search of a way out of his self-constructed trap of success will turn inevitably to a subject so rich in possibilities for self-examination and reproach. Already there have been attempts even on the level of slick fiction, Bruce Jay Friedman turning his hand to the theme in the title story of his recent collection of commercial stories, *Black Angels,* which concerns a feckless and abandoned suburbanite (this time Friedman pretends he is an Italian called Stefano, but we recognize him as our old friend, Stern) who falls into the hands of a group of Negroes who come on as incredibly cheap workmen, but in the end reveal themselves as psychiatrists preparing to bleed him to death with exorbitant fees. It is a nightmare vision rendered with all the insouciance of a joke, a blackout gag in the continuing burlesque show of suburban life.

Reading Friedman and Neugeboren and Hentoff, however, we remember the writer who began it all, the Jewish boy out of Harvard who first declared himself a White Negro, Norman Mailer—and suddenly there returns to mind the terrible and triumphant scene out of *An American Dream,* in which Stephen Rojack (himself a half-Jewish Raskolnikov crossed with James, or is it Israel, Bond) beats out the "spade" junkie with a knife for the possession of the blonde Cherry, all-American Wasplet, who stands obviously for that erotic dream of a pale Protestant America waiting to be won, a dream shared by Jew and Negro alike. Maybe we are not so sure of the boast implicit in Mailer that we Jewish boys are still capable of taking the archetypal American *shikse* out of the hands of any "spade," however well armed; but it does us good to dream so in a time of troubles. And if Mailer goes on to tell us, as he does, that the girl finally dies, that we are both, Negroes and Jews alike, left with a ghost only, a disembodied voice on the telephone—this bad news we can stand, too, after the dreamed moment of glory.

—1967

FOURTEEN

Some Notes on the Jewish Novel in English or Looking Backward from Exile

"BY THE RIVERS OF Babylon we sat down and wept . . ."; or so at least it is reported in *the* Book: the first—though by no means the last—of those Jewish books which the non-Jewish world has somehow been persuaded is its book, too. Sat down and wept, to be sure, but sang and wrote too, sang of the weeping, wrote of the singing, thus inventing the first Jewish profession, writing in exile—a permanent Jewish profession everywhere. I had thought it in America, only last year. But this year I have looked about me in search of Jewish writers in England, *real* Jewish writers, who write their Jewishness, however vestigial, and their exile, however cozy; and convince non-Jewish readers that in some sense they are Jews, too, and exiles as well, though they had not suspected it before. And I have found none. No Jewish writers in England. How can it be?

The question troubled me from the start, and so I asked those whom destiny (I have been teaching in an English University all year) had put in my power, my poor captive students. How does it happen, I demanded of them, that there is no serious, no considerable Anglo-Jewish Novel? You share with us Americans a common language, the mother-tongue, in fact, of most living Jews, who once wrote in Aramaic or Arabic or Yiddish or German, but now choose English or American or Anglo-American. Way back at the turn of the century you produced Israel Zangwill, one of the first Jewish

156

writers to adopt the new mother tongue. But though in the United States novelists like Bellow and Mailer and Malamud, poets like Allen Ginsberg, speak for all Americans, stand at the center of the scene—almost too established, too successful, so that resentment grows and anti-establishment writers begin to consider them the enemy; nothing remotely similar has happened, is happening here. And why not?

It was a foolish question, perhaps, and so deserved the silence which greeted it, as it greeted most of the misguided American questions I directed at my baffled students in those first weeks. Finally, however, I did get an answer from a girl who, until that point, had always proved more charming than articulate, but was moved at last to say, smiling benignly, "Well—They're All so Rich here, They don't have to write Books, do They?" After which it was my turn to be silent; though I suppose she was really suggesting an answer with her distancing "They" and her offhand evocation of the envious-spiteful stereotype. Maybe it is essentially that mild-as-milk, matter-of-fact anti-Semitism, which I have found everywhere in England, that has prevented Jews here from becoming spokesmen for anything except their own parochial interests, or, alternatively, slightly quaint entertainers like, say, Chaim Bermant.

For better or for worse (so at any rate it seems to me), the Jews in England, quite like the Pakistanis or the Jamaicans, or, for that matter, the Irish, are felt to be English only insofar as they seem to have ceased being Jewish; but this is the absolute opposite of the American case, in which the rule is, has been for a decade or two: the more Jewish, the more American. It is for this reason, then, that the handful of Anglo-Jewish writers of talent actually producing fiction and verse are not felt to add up to anything significant. There are novelists who happen to be Jewish but no Jewish novel.

On the other hand, there is a *female* novel in England, where certain middle-aged women (some of them irrelevantly Jewish) tend to function like certain middle-aged Jews (some of them irrelevantly female) in the United States. I do not read these English ladies often or with much pleasure, but I have enough sense of them to have composed in my head a composite portrait of the typical recent English novelist labeled, for convenience, Muriel Murdoch.

And in moments of perversity, I have tried to imagine mating her with her American opposite number, called, of course, Bernard Bellow. They are not utterly unlike, since M.M. shares with B.B. certain memories of the thirties and World War II, as well as an interest in the language of Existentialism. But her stock-in-trade is her battered sexuality rather than her disappearing ethnic identity; and even if her affairs turn out to be, like his ghetto origins, just another image for alienation, I am afraid I could never get my imaginary couple past the first strains of introduction. Perhaps the true opposite of the Jew is not (as, I seem to recall, Maurice Samuel once suggested) the Gentleman, but the Lady, or, to be quite up-to-date, the ex-Lady; and these opposites do *not* attract.

America has, at any rate, ever since the end of the War against Hitler chosen to identify itself with the Jew—quite disregarding a warning against this rapprochement issued some fifty years ago by D. H. Lawrence, who, however resolutely *not* a gentleman, was as anti-Semitic as any Englishman. Meanwhile, England has chosen to see itself as the aging lady, which means, I suppose, no match— though a transatlantic offspring is possible all the same; since in the realm of the imagination, even the refusal to mate is not a guaranteed contraceptive. But where could he go, this unwanted child of M.M. and B.B., equally unwelcome at both poles of the English-speaking world, except, perhaps, to the no man's land, the Demilitarized Zone of Canada. But if he were, in fact, there, he would be invisible from South of the Border as well as from the Other Side of the Atlantic—since, despite occasional valiant efforts to *find* Canadian literature (Edmund Wilson provides one notable recent example), it remains stubbornly unavailable to English and American readers alike.

Still, I myself have been reading Canadian books for a long time and have been variously amused, dismayed, interested and bored—but not really moved (even enough to want to register my reactions in print) except by the work of two authors, both self-exiled English-speaking Jews from Montreal, one of whom I have known for a long time now, the other of whom I have come across only quite recently: Mordecai Richler and Leonard Cohen. That they both be Jews is fair enough, proving once more that, culturally speaking, Canada is part of the American rather than the British

Commonwealth; and that they have both chosen to exile themselves from their place of birth is appropriate, too, proving once more that the America Canada is really like is always the America of three decades before.

Among us in the United States, exile, particularly to England, seems scarcely a typical strategy these days (imagine Saul Bellow or John Barth or Allen Ginsberg permanently planted in the English countryside); but for Richler it apparently provides the possibility of participating in American culture—contributing to *Commentary,* starring in the first issue of the *New American Review* —without the defensive self-consciousness he would have felt following a similar course at home. From England, at any rate, he seems to able to join, however belatedly, the extended Norman Podhoretz "family" not as a poor relation from the North, but as a distinguished foster-brother from overseas. And England, in addition, has provided him with a new subject, the subject of exile, latterday or post-romantic exile itself, rescuing him from the need to recapitulate earlier American models. *The Apprenticeship of Duddy Kravitz,* for instance, seemed to me when I first encountered it, hopelessly retrospective for all the talent that went into its making —the sort of fictional study of making it out of the ghetto appropriate for Americans only to the thirties. *Having* made it was our new subject—and Richler's, too, though he did not seem to know it at the start. Still, there was apparent in him a lust for surreal exaggeration and the grotesque, and an affinity for the atrocious—the dirty joke turned somehow horrific, the scene of terror altered somehow into absurdity—which made him, before he himself knew it, a member of the group later to be labeled Black Humorists.

Satire was his special affinity—not, to be sure, polished and urbane satire, but shrill and joyously vulgar travesty—directed, all the same, against pop culture, on the one hand, and advanced or experimental art on the other: middlebrow satire, in fact, however deliciously gross, an antigenteel defense of the genteel tradition. It is this which makes Richler so difficult a writer for *me* to come to terms with, and—by the same token—so easy a one for the guardians of official morality to accept. His most recent novel, *Cocksure,* for instance, was simultaneously published in permissive America and in restrictive England; and though it contains one episode in which it is revealed that a prim and aging schoolmarm has been blowing the top boys in her class, there has been no protest from an irate British public, and no action from the British courts which recently condemned and banned *Last Exit to Brooklyn*. Part of the explanation for this must be surely that, never mind *how,* the schoolmarm in question is re-establishing discipline and hard work in a formerly progressive school; and no true-blue Englishman wants to deny what Richler suggests: better *fellatio* than children's productions of plays by the Marquis de Sade. Besides which, in tone and language and indefinable stance Richler himself belongs to the world of mass culture (in which he has labored long, continues to support himself), so that he seems ultimately—*seems,* I think, rather than is—as harmless as *The Black and White Minstrel Show*.

It is quite another aspect of his work which makes Richler more dangerous than he seems perhaps even to himself: his concern with exile, his compulsion to define all predicaments in terms of that hopelessly Jewish concept, and his implicit suggestion that, after all, we are—every one of us—Jews. In an oddly uncharacteristic, but to me impressive, book called *A Choice of Enemies* (the structure of which reminds me disconcertingly of Graham Greene), Richler turned his cold satirical eye on certain Hollywood exiles in England, victims of the anti-Communist heresy hunts of the fifties, who, stripped of power and wealth, continue to play the old Machiavellian games which earlier they had carried on behind their mouthing of Communist pieties. And in *The Incomparable Atuk,* he deals with the fate of a Far North Eskimo in the world of Toronto pop culture, moving closer and closer to a level of farce and fantasy whose connections with reality are more like those of a Mack Sennet comedy than a novel of the late nineteenth or early twentieth century.

The Incomparable Atuk is not quite a successful book (I notice it is not even included among the earlier Richler books listed opposite the title page of *Cocksure);* but in it Richler seems to have discovered at last where the demands of his real gifts were taking him —toward ultimate, absolute burlesque, i.e., burlesque that includes finally the book itself and its author, the sort of nihilism implicit unawares in all pop art, and consciously exploited in "Pop Art," of which *Cocksure* is an example. But ultimate burlesque requires a sense of the ultimate outsider, the real victim, the true Jew, who—in the realm of Anglo-Saxondom at least—turns out to be the Anglo-Saxon: Richler's poor Mortimer Griffin, a Canadian in the world of Anglo-American T.V. and films, convinced that the Jews are thicker, the Negroes longer than he, who is cuckolded, sacked, and due to be murdered as the book closes. He has discovered before that conclusion that certain powerful Jewish entrepreneurs—in particular a bisexual monster-producer, kept alive with multiple transplants—actually manufacture out of plastic the WASP robots who are the screen idols of the world; and is—naturally enough—taken for mad by those whose peace of mind demands that they believe plastic the ultimate reality. It is a book which seems always on the verge of becoming truly obscene but stops short, alas, at the merely funny. Yet it is so close, so close—the sort of near miss that leaves permanent damage behind.

Perhaps it is close enough, then. Certainly Richler has come as near to saying how it is with us now, when the ultimate exile has proved to be success, as anyone can out of the generation which dreamed that success, at a point when being poor and excluded seemed the only real indignity. Or perhaps it is even possible to say that he has come as near as satire can under any circumstances, since satire is the weapon of one—his deepest self made by a failed father, a deprived childhood—who secretly believes himself weak. The weapon of the strong is joy, of the half-strong pathos and sentimentality; and Leonard Cohen calls on the latter, while he woos the former in hope.

He begins with certain social advantages, aside from all questions of gifts, since he was born in another generation (ten years makes all the difference), another Montreal (not the old ghetto, but suburbia which reveals its dreams as delusions); and he has sought another exile (Greece, the Island of Hydra, which is to say the remotest and most sunlit of all American Bohemias). And being of another generation, his relationship to pop culture is utterly different—not the condescension and self-inclusive scorn of one forced to earn his living in its terms and thinking of it as a kind of prostitution, against which the appropriate revenge is "art"; but the admiration of one to whom it was forbidden by finicky parents when he was a child, and who therefore cannot help believing it a source of power, a guide for redeeming "art" turned genteel. In any case, the pop art which most moves Cohen and provides not the subject so much as the mythology which informs his work is not films and television, but comic books and pop music. Superman and Ray Charles inhabit his imagination as the Hollywood Producer and the M.C. of the Panel Show inhabit Richler's. And he is quite properly, therefore, a successful writer of pop songs (his latest album recently released in England as well as America), in addition to being a poet and novelist. As a matter of fact, I find his song lyrics (in "Suzanne," for instance, and especially "The Sisters of Mercy") more valid than his book-poetry, because the former have found contemporary occasions which justify their pathos and sentimentality, whereas the latter seem moved merely by nostalgia for certain lapsed Romantic styles. He works, at any rate, not in the middlebrow arena of Richler, in which pop and *avant-garde* are felt as complementary threats, but the new post-Modernist world in which the old distinctions between low and high art, mass culture and *belles-lettres* have lapsed completely—and it is therefore, blessedly impossible to be either alienated or outrageous. Vision replaces satire in that world, which aims at transforming consciousness rather than reforming manners.

Nonetheless, Cohen has found no publisher yet in England willing to risk bringing out his extraordinary second novel, *Beautiful Losers,* since in England (particularly after the court decision against *Last Exit to Brooklyn* seemed to give official sanction to it), the art of being outraged by what is not outrageous has been highly developed. I suppose the point is that Cohen does not make dirty jokes at all, certainly not dirty jokes at the expense of what is advanced or experimental, but tries instead to blur the boundaries between the clean and the dirty, even as he has those between serious art and popular entertainment. Or, perhaps, the former is only a particular case of the latter since it is the end of "porn" as an underground, secretly relished genre which books like *Beautiful Losers* threaten. For it is to a place before or beyond the realm of the dirty book that we are taken by scenes like the terrible-lyrical one in which Cohen's two male lovers jerk each other off as they speed in an automobile toward what seems a wall of solid stone; or the terrible apocalyptic one, in which a heterosexual pair, exhausted of passion and drained of all their liquids after a bout with an erotic device called the "Danish Vibrator," rouse to find themselves confronted by Hitler naked beneath a military raincoat. Certainly, Cohen has found to render such scenes a language not gross and elegant by turns, but gross and elegant at once, a poetry of obscenity which makes condescension to him or his subjects impossible. And perhaps it is the possibility of condescension for which the English are fighting in the courts, having lost the battle everywhere else.

I should hate really to deprive anyone who really wants it of that last vestigial pleasure of class consciousness; but it seems even more unfair to rob young readers especially of the pleasures of Cohen's novel with its special blend of scholarship and paranoia, poetry and vulgarity, its intertwined stories (on one level, it recounts the death by self-torture of a seventeenth-century Indian girl converted to Christianity and pledged to chastity for Christ's sake; on the other, it tells of a polymorphous perverse triangle in twentieth-century Montreal moving through joy toward madness and death), and its final vision of redemption, through the emergence of the New Jew—a saving remnant who, Cohen assures us, does not necessarily have to be Jewish at all, but probably does have to be American. It is a possibility in which I find myself believing, in part, of course because I want to (which is always more than half the battle), but in part because the evidence is *there,* in the text and texture of *Beautiful Losers* itself; so that it is not merely prophecy or an idle boast when Cohen writes toward the book's close: "Hey, cried a New Jew, laboring on the lever of the Broken Strength Test. Hey. Somebody's making it!"

—1968

Negro and Jew

THIS IS A MOMENT for questions, new questions or old ones newly posed, a moment when answers seem impertinent—which is, perhaps, why fiction (a method of posing questions without troublesome question marks) seems the most promising method of attacking the problem of Negro-Jewish hostility. I am thinking of such books as Norman Mailer's *An American Dream,* Nat Hentoff's *Call the Keeper,* and Jay Neugeboren's *Big Man,* as well as (hopefully) my own *The Last Jew in America.* In a strange way it has now become incumbent on the Jewish writer to re-imagine the Negro in terms which will escape the old WASP clichés, sentimental and vicious, and the recent even more soupy and hysterical Spade ones. Eventually, of course, the Negro writer himself will have to invent the New Negro as Harriet Beecher Stowe, Mark Twain, D. W. Griffith and Faulkner have invented the Old Negro. But Jews will apparently have to deal with him in the moment of transition, since the current crop of Negro novelists is fumbling the job: Ellison remaining stubbornly old-fashioned on this score, Baldwin caught between the exigencies of his poetic talent and his political commitment, LeRoi Jones the victim of his own anguish and *mishigas.* But the Jewish writer's assumption of this task can prove in the end only one more possible source of misunderstanding and tension between the two groups.

Some relevant questions then—and all which follows is a series of questions even when passion or strategy leads me to omit the question marks. Would not the proper title for an article on this subject be "Thou shalt not honor the poor man in his cause"—to remind the present-day enlightened Jew of certain therapeutic anti-liberal elements in his own tradition: a priestly admonition that might have protected him in the thirties from illusions about the working class and its parties (but did not); and might now serve as an antidote against delusive hopes about Negroes and their organizations (but probably will not). Or maybe it would be better—in light of my own continuing concerns—to use the title *An End to (Another) Innocence;* since the liberal tradition in America—to which the Jewish intellectual has attached himself, which, indeed, he has all but pre-empted—insists on stumbling from one innocence to another with appropriate bouts of self-recrimination between. It is not mere "white backlash" (the very term is a buttress of naïveté on the defensive) but simple wisdom (what used to be called "good sense") to notice that, like all such movements, the Civil Rights Movement is becoming, had to become with the beginnings of success, self-seeking, self-deceiving, self-defeating—devoted not to a search for justice but to the pursuit of power. But the liberals (the *Jewish* liberals, as Negro critics like to say) will be the last to admit this; since the liberal is a man who can drown in the same river twice—which is, let me be clear, his glory as well as his folly, the function of an incredible generosity of spirit which fades imperceptibly into willful stupidity: a combination, mythologically speaking, of *yiddishe hertz* and *goyishe kop.*

Why not continue to speak mythologically then; for mythology seems the basic way into the problem of Jewish-Negro hostility— which turns out not to exist sociologically at all, i.e., not *consciously* (using the methods of the behavioral sciences, investigators keep discovering to their own satisfaction and the confusion of the rest of us, that Negroes really love, respect, and honor Jews) but only preconsciously, on the level of legend and nightmare.

What, in fact, are the mythologies at work, first in the minds of Negroes concerning Jews and then in the minds of Jews concerning Negroes? "Sub-minds" would be a more precise way of naming the locus of myths: and is it not well to remind ourselves in this regard of the differing weights of mind and submind, conscious and preconscious factors in the case of Negro and Jew? It is no secret, surely, that in America the Jewish Community has largely committed itself to a life of logos, a cultivation of the ego and the whole Gutenburg bit whose demise Marshall McLuhan has been quite un-Jewishly predicting; while the Negro community in large part continues to live (even to make its living) in the world of subliteracy, unrationalized impulse, and free fantasy.

Do not Negroes, in any event, tend to begin with the WASP racist mythology (endorsing it in self-hatred, or inverting it in impotent rebellion) which divides the world into two ethnic-mythic segments only: White and Colored; and which further assumes that the distinction is hierarchal, corresponding roughly to higher and lower. The deep Jewish ethnic-mythic division, on the other hand, is threefold, as the legend of the three sons of Noah reminds us. As descendants of Shem, we were once taught, we have *two* hostile and inferior brothers, Ham and Japheth. The Negro, committed to his simpler mythology, tends to regard the Jew either as a Colored Man who is deviously passing as White; or a goddamned White Man pretending, for reasons hard to fathom, to the fate of the excluded Colored Man. The Jew, meanwhile, is struggling with the vestigial sense of being a third thing, neither-either, however one says it; and he therefore thinks of himself (his kind of awareness driving him compulsively from feeling to thinking) as being free to "pass" in either direction, in a world which oddly insists that he identify himself with one group of strangers or another, Hamitic or Japhetic. And he knows that historically segments of his people have done both (some first pretending to be White, then becoming prisoners of their pretense; some following the opposite strategy): that in Israel, for instance, it is possible to observe these two groups, "Black Jews" and "White Jews," in open conflict. He is, therefore, baffled as well as resentful when he discovers himself denominated "White" without choice and made the victim in a Black-White race riot; just as he was once baffled as well as resentful to discover himself linked without choice to Negroes in being excluded from White clubs and hotels and restaurants. And he is doubly baffled and resentful when the Negro switches from hating him as White to despising him in a mode imitated from those earlier-arrived North European Americans who thought themselves so much Whiter than he.

How can the Jew help seeing Negro anti-Semitism as a kind of culture-climbing, an illegitimate attempt to emulate WASP style —and, inevitably, a belated and misguided attempt; since the

WASPs are abandoning the racist attitudes to which the Negro aspires at the very moment he is assimilating them. Even Hitler, certain more ignorant or frantic Negroes tend to think of as just another White Man—rather more efficient than most, though not
quite efficient enough in eliminating his Jew-enemies—and thus
they have not felt shamed out of their anti-Semitism by the rise and
fall of Nazism, as their WASP opposite numbers (who cannot help
feeling Hitler in some sense one of them) have tended to be. It is
especially unassimilated, unassimilable Jews, Jews who do not even
seem to want to look like all other Americans, who stir the fury of
Negro hoods—say, Hasidim with their beards, *peyes* and gabardines.

At the deepest mythological level, is it not the Jewish religion,
finally, as well as the Jewish ethnic inheritance which bugs the Negroes? Certainly this would be understandable enough; for insofar
as they are Christians, fundamentalist, evangelical Protestants, do
they not inherit the simple-minded anti-Jewish mythology of the
Gospels (which Catholics long had the good grace to keep out of
the hands of subliterates) with its simple-minded melodrama of
"our" Christ killed by "the Jews"? And do not Negroes in particular possess the additional sentimental myth of Simon the Cyrenean
—kindly Negro by the wayside—who helped Jesus bear his cross as
the Jews hooted and howled for his blood? And insofar as they are
becoming Muslim (Why could not the first attempt of the ill-fated
founder of that movement to establish a Black Judaism have succeeded?), are they not obsessed by the legendary notion of the
"Evil Jacob," Israel the Usurper—as well as the myth of Isaac before him doing poor Ishmael out of his heritage? And as Muslims,
do not they (along with the members of other non-Mohammedan
Afro organizations) identify themselves with an Arab-African
anti-Jewish political mythology, which leads them to consider Jews,
in America as well as Israel, even wickeder than the rest of the de-
praved "hoojis"? Are not both Christianity and Islam, finally, being
offshoots of a more primitive Judaism, subject to spasms of a kind
of collective sibling rivalry, which passes over on occasion into frat-
ricidal strife? And is not the *shul*-goer or temple-attending Jew
caught once more in the old bind between the Christian Negro for
whom he is not (spiritually) White enough—not sufficiently
washed in the Blood of the Lamb—and the Muslim Negro for

whom he is not (mythologically) Black enough—not far enough removed from the White Man's God?

It is not, however, only the worshipers of Christ or the followers of Mohammed among the Negroes who are possessed by anti-Jewish mythologies. The hippiest and most advanced Negroes, seculaı as they may seem to themselves, are committed to a myth system—the Beat Religion, let's call it for the purposes of quick identification, most recent form of an old Romantic anti-Church. And does that Church not necessarily, in view of its archetypal antecedents, see the Negro as the embodiment of (admired) impulse and irrationality, the Jew as the incarnation of (despised) sublimation and rationality? About these matters I have written at some length before; and have thought about them long enough not to be surprised at recent efforts at expelling Allen Ginsberg from the True Church (a kind of apostle to the Beat Gentiles, or maybe better, a Trotsky of the Hip revolution—his position is more than a little anomalous). No one, at any rate, need pretend astonishment when he hears the cry from a Negro at the back of a room in which Robert Creeley is reading aloud, "This is a poem for Allen Ginsberg" —"Hey, man, when you going to stop talking about those Jew poets?" Is it not a rule of the mythological literary life in America that when the Negro is up, the Jew is down? What was true in the twenties is true once again as the Jewish thirties, forties, and early fifties recede from us. Who can serve two masters, after all? One must choose between Saul Bellow and LeRoi Jones, Jerusalem (well, the Northwest side of Chicago at any rate) and Harlem (well, let's make it Newark's Third Ward). Mythological as well as historical factors, that is to say, have determined the fact that certain Hippies at the present moment find themselves protesting a Jewish Literary Establishment ("Norman Podhoretz's floating ghetto," one in-group joke calls it) in the name of a movement whose reigning figures are archetypal *goyim* like Charles Olson, Norman O. Brown and Marshall McLuhan. Jewish writers, from Mailer to Nat Hentoff, may try to escape the mythological hang-up by redefining themselves as imaginary or "White Negroes" (the very term was, of course, invented by a Jew)—just as their more political brethren have tried to assimilate to a world which mythologically rejects them by linking arms with Negroes in protests and demonstrations. But though young Jews have an affinity not only for protest but for folksongs, jazz, and marijuana (how much more readily they assimilate to pot than to the Paleface medicine of whiskey), the whole syndrome, they have trouble making it across the legendary line—remain always in danger of being told that they cannot *really* commit themselves to the Movement, cannot *really* make authentic jazz, cannot *really* sing the blues. The point is that other mythological demands are being made on them—to play the false liberal, or "Mr. Goldberg" or, ultimately, the super-ego in one or another currently unfashionable form.

So much—for the moment—about the Negro or Negroizing mythologies of the Jew; though I suppose a word at least demands to be said about the "Black Socialism" (the term antedates its adoption by actual Blacks), that presumably revolutionary anti-Semitism which poor Negroes have inherited from White workers, *lumpen* proletarians, peasants and "red-necks." This view (to which Leo Frank was once a victim) sees the Jew as rich, powerful, devious, behind the scenes if not at the centers of power—a Boss, in short. But this view tends to become less and less influential as the leading elements of the Negro Movement become prosperous or mobile and educated enough to afford overt anti-Semitism. It is real enough, to be sure, but is it not finally a vestige, as old-fashioned, which is to say, as peripheral in the current situation as the remnants among the aging Jewish bourgeoisie of the simple-minded anti-Negroism appropriate to our social-climbing days: the contempt of the still insecure Jewish housewife for the *schwarze* who cleaned for her, or the Jewish marginal small businessman for his Negro janitor, or the underpaid Jewish salesman for his Negro instalment customer? Do we not enjoy rehashing such elementary prejudices, long after we have made it in a way which renders them irrelevant, precisely because they are no longer urgent; and leaving them, we would have to confront relationships much more difficult to analyze or confess?

Almost as familiar, and therefore quite as ritually satisfying to discuss yet one more time, are certain good old Freudian notions—long since lapsed into semi-popular mythology—about the Negro: the projection onto the Negro male, for instance, of the sadist nightmares about his own women dreamed by the white male, etc.,

etc. These have always been rather confused as far as Jews in America are concerned, by the fact that Jews themselves have played similar mythological-sexual roles in WASP erotic fantasies; and in Norman Mailer's last novel one can see enacted in the form of comic melodrama a kind of contest between his (half) Jewish hero and a particularly potent Spade to see which one will possess the blond all-American *shikse*—which, mythologically speaking, amounts, I suppose, to an argument about which one of us she is dreaming these days. More interesting, and more dangerous to broach, are questions about the role of homosexual rather than heterosexual fantasies in the earlier stages of the Civil Rights Movement. I am not referring to the fact that there has been a strange confluence of the Homosexual Rebellion (the emergence of queer America from underground to the daylight world) and the Negro Movement; but rather to the influence on that Movement of the old antifemale dream of a pure love between males, colored and white, so crucial to our classic literature in the United States. I myself can report having heard several times in various forms from young civil rights workers the cry, so authentically American it was hard at first to believe: "Oh, Christ, things were great when just us buddies Black and White were fighting it out together; but these White chicks are just down here to get laid."

It seems to me, however, that none of these sexual concerns, deep as they may go, are as important at the moment as certain political mythologies. What chiefly exacerbates relations between Negroes and Jews, as far as Jews are concerned, is the persistence among them of the mythology of Liberal Humanism. This troublesome myth system, derived in part from Old Testament sources, most highly developed in modern Anglo-Saxondom, and picked up again in that world by emancipated Jewish intellectuals, includes the following articles of faith: that all men desire freedom and full human status and deny that freedom and status to others only when it has been refused to them; that equality of opportunity leads to maximum self-fulfillment and social well-being; that the oppressed and the injured have been so ennobled by their oppression and injury that they are morally superior to their masters; that all men desire literacy and suffrage—and can exercise those privileges equally well when granted them; that all the foregoing are not the parochial belief of a tiny minority of mankind over a minute span of time, but what all men have always believed, or would have believed given the opportunity. Intertwined with this credo—though not as often avowed as that credo itself—is the Whig Myth of History which sees freedom slowly broadening down from precedent to precedent, country to country and ethnic group to ethnic group. The Jews have always (since their exit from the ghetto and entry into the West, at least) considered themselves more qualified than anyone, less compromised than anyone because of their historical situation certainly, to preach this doctrine. They have felt especially righteous in respect to the application of these principles to the Negroes in the United States, since they were not as a group involved in the enslavement of the Negro, and they know themselves to have long been involved in Civil Rights Movements in numbers all out of proportion to the percentage of the total population which they represent. No Negro ever died for a Jewish cause, Jews tell themselves; but some of our boys have died for Negro rights.

How utterly unprepared they have been, therefore, to find a growing number of Negroes rejecting not only their credo but them in particular as its messengers—spurning in short the whole body of "Jewish Liberalism." "Hear our message and be saved," they cry only a little condescendingly and are dismayed to hear in return: "All we want from you white mothers (or alternatively, Jew mothers) is to get off our backs and out of our road!" Yet worse, much worse, is the fact that the Negroes, whatever their avowed credo, challenge by their very existence a basic article of the Liberal Faith: equality of opportunity will not grant very many of them, brutalized by long brainwashing and bred by a kind of unnatural selection, a decent life or the possibility of prosperity. What they demand, not so much by what they say as by how they are, how they test, how they perform, is *special privilege* rather than equality if they are to make it at all in the very world in which the Jews have so preeminently flourished. And what a shame and embarrassment that some men (i.e., most Jews) have done so well under conditions in which certain fellow-humans seem bound to do ill. What can survive of liberal mythology in the face of this? Is "liberalism," then, only a camouflage for a special sort of privilege, a code by which the peoples who alone have long lived with the alphabet can triumph over all others?

Marxism, especially in its more brutal Bolshevik versions, has long offered an alternative mythology to that of liberalism; but so many intellectual Jews now sufficiently advanced into middle age to have become its spokesmen have been there before. Some, indeed, are alive and articulate at the moment who have lived through the loss of three religions: first Orthodoxy itself, then Stalinism or Trotskyism, finally enlightened liberalism; and for them, what lies ahead but despair? But for the young, and the politically obtuse who remember nothing and have learned nothing, it seems possible, even imperative—in order to justify or explain black violence, black know-nothingism, black racism—to fall back once more on the mythology of an already once-discredited anti-liberal Bolshevik "Humanism." Certainly, there is superficial reassurance at least in the simple-minded theory that the whole vexed problem is "economic"—and that the last vestiges of Black Racism will disappear (like anti-Semitism in the Soviet Union? a nagging voice demands) only after the major means of production have been appropriated by the People's State. But how can a thinking man live by the mythology of a God who died in the declining thirties? And how especially can a Jew come to terms with the fate of his own people by applying a Marxist mythology which denies the Jewishness of the Jews—as is, after all, appropriate to a secular religion invented in large part by recusant Jews. To be sure, any and all "Jewish problems" immediately disappear when the real reference of the adjective is denied; but this is a semantic solution which cannot conceal the fact that actual Jews are being harried and threatened. And if proof is needed that this semantic strategy is not only a lie but an offense, one need only see Peter Weiss' current play, *The Investigation,* that obscene parody of what happened at Auschwitz, from which "the Jews" have been expunged, even as a name to be spoken aloud.

No, more attractive to me than yesterday's defunct mythology —more valid for all the self-pity easily attached to it—is the more ancient mythology which insists that the ultimate villains of history define themselves finally and essentially by their attitude toward the

Jews; and that all enemies of the Jews (with whatever pious slogans and whatever history of suffering they begin) are enemies to the good of mankind, whether they be black, brown, yellow, or white —Haman or Hitler or the CORE leader rising to scream that Hitler should have done a better job of getting rid of us. "Not in one generation alone, but in every generation they have risen up to destroy us," the ritual phrase in the Passover Haggadah runs; and it continues on to reassure us that God has always delivered us out of the hands of our enemies. But what about the hands of our presumed, even our real, allies? And what can we expect anyhow in these dark days when God is dead and only the devil survives: the devil still identified by Ku Kluxers with Negroes, and by some Negroes with the Jews? What does the devil's devil do in a world without God, or even gods?

Despair? Make jokes? Pray to the void? Confess that nothing can be done? That by a joke of history the amends that *must* be made to the Negroes (for indignities for which the Jews bear little or no guilt) must, alas, necessarily do harm to the Jews? That it is our turn again, or really on this continent at long last? Sometimes I feel this way and am tempted toward desolation; until, looking out into the streets, the schoolyards, the coffeehouses, I find my heart leaping up at the sight of young couples linked arm in arm. And I think our daughters will save us, love (not big theoretical, but small sexual love) will save us. I remember a year or two ago riding a plane to Jerusalem and being told by the man seated beside me, who worked for a Jewish adoption agency, that the number of illegitimate Negro babies being produced by Jewish girls was mounting spectacularly. And were there also, I asked, legitimate ones, *even* legitimate ones? But I did not listen for the answer, knowing it was yes, and not quite sure why I needed confirmation. What sunders us may not be first of all but is last of all a sexual taboo; and that taboo is every day being broken, with or without benefit of clergy, Christian or Jewish; and its breaking is the beginning (though *only* the beginning) of the end.

So naturally a new mythology is being invented, appropriate to that new solution; though like all new myths this one, too, contains within it one very old, indeed, the myth of the Jewish Daughter, Hadassah (renamed Esther, which is to say, Ashtoreth) dancing naked for our salvation before the Gentile King. I sat the other day eavesdropping on the conversation of a group of very young white girls—most of them pretty, blonde daughters of Jews with black boyfriends, discussing what they would do when the first race riots broke out in Buffalo. And one of them suggested that they march between the two opposed packs, Black and White, carrying signs which read: MAKE LOVE NOT WAR. It was elegant and vain as the loveliest dream; and I am old and cynical enough, after all, to know it; as I know how much there is dark and desperate even in their young love, and as I realize how much in marriage itself (for some few of them *will* marry their Negro boyfriends, I am sure) is a problem rather than a solution. To make matters worse, I had just been reading in the *East Village Other* a statement by a Negro poet, who not so long before had been able to write that he had "married a Jewish Lady to escape Bohemia," that Jewish girls only married Negroes in order to emasculate them. And I was aware that it was his paranoid and sinister mythology which operated in the tensions that made headlines day after day; but I knew that the counter-mythology of those young girls had power to move men, too. I, at least, prefer to live in its hope rather than the Negro poet's despair, convinced of its superiority to all the weary mythologies of mere politics. The disillusionment it will inevitably breed at least still lies ahead, and (if I am lucky) I may not live so long.

—1966

SIXTEEN

Master of Dreams:
The Jew in a Gentile World

If there were dreams to sell,
Merry and sad to tell,
And the crier rung the bell,
What would you buy?

T. L. BEDDOES

"AND JOSEPH DREAMED a dream," the Book of the Jews tells us, "and he told it his brethren: and they hated him yet the more." It is the beginning of a myth whose ending we all know, the opening of a larger dream which a whole community has dreamed waking and aloud for nearly three thousand years. But it is unique among communal dreams, this myth of Joseph and his descent into Egypt; for it is the dream of the dreamer, a myth of myth itself. More specifically (or maybe I only mean more Jewishly), it is the dreamer's own dream of how, dreaming, he makes it in the waking world; the myth of myth making it in the realm of the nonmythic; an archetypal account of the successful poet and the respected shrink, the Jewish artist and the Jewish doctor—hailed in the Gentile world, first by the Gentiles themselves, and as a consequence by their hostile brethren, their fellow-Jews.

I might have hit upon the meaning of the Joseph story in any number of ways, reflecting on the Biblical text itself, or reading Thomas Mann's true but tedious retelling of the tale in *Joseph and His Brethren;* but I did not. And only after I had begun my own

ruminations did I come on Isaac Bashevis Singer's exegesis, in a little story called "The Strong Ones," in which he remembers the
strange resentment of his childhood friends after he had first revealed to them his secret desire to become a writer: "And even
though I asked how I had offended them, they behaved like Joseph's brothers and could not answer amicably. . . . What was it
they envied? My dreams. . . ." But the archetypal beginning implies
the archetypal ending; and just as mysteriously as they had rejected
him, Singer's comrades end by asking his forgiveness: "It reminded
me of Joseph and his brothers. *They* had come to Joseph to buy
grain, but why had my friends come to me? Since I had not become
Egypt's ruler, they were not required to bow down to the earth. I
had nothing to sell but new dreams."

Actually it was a chance phrase in a most *goyish* poet which
provided me with a clue to the meanings I am pursuing here, a
verse in the Sixth Satire of Juvenal, where—describing the endless
varieties of goods on sale in Rome, wares especially tempting, he
tells us, to women—he remarks that "for a few pennies" one can
buy any dream his heart desires "from the Jews." *From the Jews!*
It was those few words which fired my imagination with their
offhand assumption that dream-pedlary is a Jewish business, that
my own people have traditionally sold to the world that commodity
so easy to scorn and so difficult to do without: the stuff of dreams.
And I found myself reflecting in wonder on the strange wares that
have been in the course of Western History Jewish monopolies, real
or presumed: preserved mummy, love philtres, liquid capital, cut
diamonds, old clothes—Hollywood movies; which brought me almost up to date.

Moving backward in time, however, in reversion from such uncomfortable contemporaneity, I found myself in *Mizraim,* face to
face with the archetypal ancestor of all Jewish dreamers, with that
Joseph whom his brothers hailed mockingly, saying, "Behold, here
comes the Master of Dreams," and whom they cast into the pit,
crying out, "And then we shall see what will become of his
dreams." But we *know* what, in fact, did become of those self-flat-
tering dreams of that papa's spoiled darling. And how hard it is to
believe that there was ever a *first* time when the envious brothers
did not know in their deepest hearts what the event would be: how

Joseph, after he had ceased to dream himself, would discover that his own dreams of glory had prepared him to interpret the dreams of others, and how, interpreting them, he would achieve the wish revealed in his own.

Not, however, until he had gone down into Egypt, becoming in that absolutely alien world an absolute orphan, a Lost Son. When the Jew dreams himself in the Gentile world, it is as the preferred offspring of Jacob, which is to say, of Israel—betrayed by his brethren, but loving them still, forgiving all. When the Gentile dreams the Jew in his midst, on the other hand, he dreams him as the vengeful and villainous Father: Shylock or Fagin, the Bearded Terror threatening some poor full-grown *goy* with a knife, or inducting some guileless Gentile kid into a life of crime. But Shylock and Fagin are shadows cast upon the Christian world by that First Jewish Father, Abraham, who is to them circumcizer and sacrificer rolled into one—castrator, in short.

In the deep Jewish imagination, however, Abraham is seen always not at the moment of intended sacrifice, but the moment after —releasing his (only ritually) threatened Son to become himself a Father, and the Father of a Father, to beget Jacob who will beget Joseph. Abraham *and* Isaac *and* Jacob: these constitute that paternal triad which possesses the mythic memory of the Jews. And beyond them there is for us no further Father, only Our Boy, Joseph, who never becomes (mythically speaking) a Father at all—only makes good, i.e., provides salvation for the Gentiles and *nachas* for his own progenitor.

The Gentiles cannot afford the luxury of *our* Joseph, however, having an archetypal Son of their own, who denies his actual Jewish father ("Let the dead bury their dead"), called—appropriately enough—Joseph, too. How like and unlike the figure of the first Joseph is to that Gentiles' Son of the Father, the mythicized Jesus Christ, whose very Jewishness is finally sloughed off in the exportable archetype he becomes. Not for *our* Beloved Son a crucifixion and a translation to glory only after death. Our Dreamer, too, may begin by leaving his father's house on a mission to the Gentiles; but the temptations he must resist are the temptations of this world not the next. Specifically, he must elude not the clutch of Satan but the grasping fingers of the Gentile woman who lusts for him; and survive the slander with which she punishes his rejection of her alien charms. And his reward for virtue is to become a success in this world, the unredeemed here and now (not some New Heaven and New Earth, where he will sit at the right hand of Power), ruled over only by the powers-that-be: those fickle Pharaohs whose favor depends on his providing for them the good dreams they cannot dream for themselves, and therapeutically explaining away the bad dreams they cannot keep from dreaming.

And this means that the archetypal Jewish Son, in whatever *Mizraim* he finds himself, performs not only the function of the artist but also of the Doctor. My Son the Artist, my Son the Doctor —it is the latter which the tradition especially celebrates, the bad jokes recall in mockery; but in the tradition, the two—artist and doctor—are finally essentially one. In life, however, they may be, for all their affinities, split into separate persons, distinct and even hostile: in our own era, for instance, Sigmund Freud, on the one hand, and Franz Kafka, on the other, which is to say, the Healer and the Patient he could not have healed, since he is another, an alternative version of himself. The voice which cries, "Physician, heal thyself!" speaks always in irony rather than hope. Yet both Healer and Patient are, in some sense, or at least aspire to become, Joseph.

How eminently appropriate, then, that Kafka (first notable Jewish Dreamer of a cultural period in which the Jews of the Western World were to thrive like Joseph in Egypt, but also to be subject to such terror as the descendants of Joseph later suffered at the hands of a Pharaoh who knew him not) should have called his fictional surrogate, his most memorable protagonist, by the mythological name of Joseph. This time around, however, Joseph is specified a little, becoming—with the addition of the author's own final initial—Joseph K., a new Joseph sufficient unto his day. This Joseph, at any rate, along with the fable through which he moves, embodied for two or three generations of writers to follow (real Jews and imaginary ones, Americans and Europeans, White men and Black) not only a relevant dream-vision of terror, but also the techniques for rendering that dream in the form that Freud had meanwhile taught us was most truly dreamlike: with a nighttime illogic, at once pellucid and dark, and a brand of wit capable of revealing our most arcane desires.

Yet despite the borrowed name of his surrogate-hero, Kafka could no longer imagine a Happy Ending for either that character or himself, since he no longer dreamed himself the Beloved of his father, but an outcast, unworthy and rejected. In what has become perhaps the best known, since it is, surely, the most available, of his stories, *Metamorphosis,* his Joseph protagonist becomes a vermin in his father's eyes. And we are left with the question: how did the lovely boy in his coat-of-many-colors turn into a loathsome insect, the advisor at the royal ear into a baffled quester, an outsider barred forever from the Courts of the Mighty? But the answer to this question Kafka's own works, whatever difficult pleasure or stimulating example they may provide, do not themselves render up —not even the private and agonized "Letter to My Father," nor that final story, in which Joseph is altered in sex, demoted to Josephine, the Songstress. And the relation of the mouse-artist to the Mice-Nation (i.e., the Jews) is treated with uncustomary explicitness: "But the people, quietly, without showing any disappointment . . . can absolutely only make gifts, never receive them, not even from Josephine. . . . She is a tiny episode in the eternal history of our people, and our people will get over the loss."

No, if we would really discover what went wrong with Kafka's relationship to his own father, which is to say, to Israel itself (he who never mentioned the word "Jew" in his published work) which that father represented, or more generally to his inherited past—to history and myth—we must turn back to another Master of Dreams: the Doctor who preceded and survived the Artist: a latter-day *Baal-ha-chalamoth* (in the sense this time of interpreter rather than dreamer), Sigmund Freud, or better, Dr. Freud. Only at this moment, as we pass into a regime of rulers who know not Joseph, have we begun to outgrow our own dependence on that Healer, to learn to see him stripped of his clinical pretenses and assimilated to the ancient myth.

And mythologically speaking, he is, of course, an *alter ego* of Franz Kafka—or more precisely, of Joseph K.—one who, like the Biblical Joseph and his namesake, descended into the abyss of ridicule and shame for the sake of his vision; then was lifted up and acclaimed a culture-hero: a Saviour of the non-Jewish world which had begun by maligning and rejecting him. Certainly, it is as a solver of dreams that Freud first attracted public notice, with that book born just as the twentieth century was being born, *The Interpretation of Dreams.* Like an artist, he himself tells us—though the comparison did not occur to him—he was granted in that book an unearned illumination, on which he was to draw for the rest of his days. "Insights such as this," he wrote much later, toward the end of his life, "fall to one's lot but once in a lifetime."

And publishing the first fruits of that illumination, he prefaced it with a quotation reflecting his sense of how monumental and monstrous a task he was beginning to undertake: *"Flectere si nequeo Superos, Acheronta movebo."* If I cannot influence the Gods above, I will set the world below in motion—set Hell in motion, he means really, but he chooses to call it "Acheron," to draw on Classical rather than Hebrew mythology, perhaps because he realizes how Faustian, Satanic, blasphemous his boast finally is. And he further clarifies what he means by quoting, in the Foreword which immediately follows, Aristotle's dictum (once more the source is our other, non-Jewish antiquity) that "the dream is not God-sent but of demonic origin." But precisely in his turning from the supernal to the infernal interpretation of dreams, Freud declares himself a true modern, which is to say, quite another sort of Joseph; though the first Joseph, to be sure, began his journey toward success with a descent into the pit.

Unlike the original Joseph, however (for whom there could be no Happy Ending unless his father survived to relish his triumph), Freud could not begin his Acherontic descent until after the death of his father—called Jacob, too, by one of those significant "accidents" which Freud himself would have been the first to point out in the case of another, but on which he never commented in his own. He could not even make the preliminary trip down, much less the eventual trip up, until his darkest wish-dream had been, in guilt and relief, achieved: not to do his rival siblings down in the eyes of his father, but to be delivered of that father—his last tie to the Jewish past—and thus be freed to become an Apostle to the Gentiles, a counselor at the Court of his own doomed Emperor. Yet, before releasing his published book to the Gentile world, or even lecturing on its substance at the Gentile University of Vienna, Freud rehearsed it in one lecture at the Jewish Academic Reading Hall, and two (however incredible it may seem) before that most bourgeois of Jewish Fraternal Organizations, the B'nai Brith—tried out his vision, that is to say, before the assembled representatives of the community to which his dead father had belonged.

Yet, despite the pieties with which he hedged his blasphemy about, Freud's Acherontic "insight" failed at first to impress either the world out of which he was trying to escape, or the one to which he aspired. The handful of reviews his book got responded to it condescendingly, lumping it with old-fashioned "Dream Books" for the ignorant and the superstitious; and it sold, during the first two years after publication, some 350 copies, scarcely any in the next five. But this is hardly to be wondered at since, to Jew and Gentile alike, Freud was proposing a radically new myth of the relation of sons to fathers, of the present to the past: a myth whose inversion of the Joseph legend never occurred to him in those terms at all. What is involved is not merely the flight from Hebrew mythology in general, which we noticed in regard to the epigraph and Foreword to *The Interpretation of Dreams,* but something much more particular.

After all, one figure out of the Old Testament did come eventually to possess the imagination of Freud and to occupy him on the level of full consciousness: the figure of Moses, whose very name —as Freud carefully points out—means in Egyptian "Son," with the patronymic suppressed and whose own fleshly father, Amram, plays no part in his myth, is not even named at the center of the tale. Surely Freud loved Moses because he would brook no father at all, Hebrew or Egyptian or Midianite, killing the surrogate for the Egyptian King who had fostered him, running off from Jethro, the father of the *shikse* he had married, and—most reluctant of Jews—refusing to have his own son circumcised until the Angel of the Lord (so runs the apocryphal extension of the story) had swallowed him from his head down to his testicles. Joseph, however, Freud does not ever mention; though as an old, old man, he wrote once—to his own son naturally—"I sometimes compare myself to the old Jacob whom in his old age his children brought to Egypt. . . ." (And not even this time did he pause to note that in becoming "Jacob," he was becoming his own father.)

In his great pioneering work, however, it is neither Jacob nor Joseph nor Moses himself whom Freud evokes, but a mythological *goy,* two mythological *goyim* out of the dreams of the Gentiles. How casually, how almost inadvertently he calls up King Oedipus and Prince Hamlet side by side in what purports to be a casual three-page digression. Compelling the deep nightmare of fathers and sons dreamed by the Western World from the fifth century before Christ to the seventeenth after his death to give up its secret: "It may be that we were all destined to direct our first sexual impulses toward our mothers and our first impulses of hatred and violence toward our fathers; our dreams convince us that we were. . . ." How calm and objective he keeps his tone, as if the "we" were more impersonal than confessional. Yet everyone knows these days that *The Interpretation of Dreams* was not the product of a sudden revelation alone, but also of a painful self-analysis, into which the death of his father had impelled Freud to plunge and from which he liked to think of himself as having emerged healed.

Unlike Kafka's *Letter to My Father,* Freud's great antipaternal work is a solution, not an exacerbation, or so at least he claimed. In him (it is his proudest boast, and we believe it), obsession is turned into vision, guilt into knowledge, *trauma* into *logos;* while in Kafka, the end is paralysis, a kind of lifelong castration, memorialized by the incomplete and bloody stumps of his most ambitious works. Freud's major works are finished—their completion as much a part of their final meaning as the incompletion of Kafka's was of his. Nonetheless, between them, Kafka and Freud, the crippled poet and the triumphant savant (for, finally, not even a measure of the worldly success of Joseph was denied to the father of psychoanalysis), have helped to determine the shape of Jewish-American writing in the first half of the twentieth century—the shape of the tradition from within which (at the moment of its imminent demise) I write of them both.

From the two, our writers have learned their proper function: to read in the dreams of the present the past which never dies and the future which is always to come; and they have, therefore, registered their vision in a form which wavers between the parable and the discursive essay, art and science. For though the means of the Jewish-American writers from Nathanael West to Norman Mailer are poetic and fictional, their ends are therapeutic and prophetic. Their outer ear may attend to the speech of their contemporaries, in the realist's hope of catching out life as it passes; but their inner ear hears still the cry of Freud: "I am proposing to show that dreams are capable of interpretation." And their characteristic tone is born of the tension between the Kafka-esque wail of *"Oi veh!"* and the Freudian shout of *"Eureka!"*

That tone is established once and for all in the work of Nathanael West, in whom begins (however little the critics may have suspected it in his own time) the great take-over by Jewish-American writers of the American imagination—our inheritance from certain Gentile predecessors, urban Anglo-Saxons and midwestern provincials of North European origin—of the task of dreaming aloud the dreams of the whole American people. How fitting, then, that West's first book—published in 1931, at the point when the first truly Jewish decade in the history of our cultural life was beginning —be called *The Dream Life of Balso Snell* and that it turn out to be, in fact, a fractured and dissolving parable of the very process by which the emancipated Jew enters into the world of Western Culture.

Balso himself gets in by penetrating through the asshole that symbol of tradition and treacherous conquest, "the famous wooden horse of the Greeks." West makes his point with some care, perhaps a little too insistently for subtlety's sake: not only is it the Trojan horse that alone gets us into the beleaguered city; but for us Jews, just to make it into the horse in the first place is a real problem—since, after all, it was built for Greeks. We do not need Balso to tell us that there are only three possible openings, three entryways into any horse, even the most fabulous of beasts; but which way is for us we do not know in advance, and this he is prepared to explain, reporting of his hero, our thirties representative: "The mouth was beyond his reach, the navel provided a cul-de-sac, and so, forgetting his dignity, he approached the last. O Anus Mirabilis!" It is a lovely, an inevitable pun—and not only in 1931, since in any age, the Jewish Dream Peddler must, like Balso, "forget his dignity" to get inside. Not for him, the High Road to Culture *via* the "horse's mouth," nor the mystical way of "contemplating the navel"; only the "Acherontic" Freudian back entrance: the anal-sexual approach. "Tradesmen enter by the rear."

For West's Balso, at any rate, the strategy works; in a moment, he is transformed from outsider to insider, but he does not like it after all. God knows what he had imagined would be waiting for him in the belly of the horse; what he discovers in fact is that it is "inhabited solely by writers in search of an audience," all Josephs and no Pharaohs. And the approval of other approval-seekers is exactly what he neither needs nor wants, though for a while he pursues one of their number, "a slim young girl" called Mary McGeeney, who has written a novel "in the manner of Richardson," the Great WASP Father of the *genre*. It is not as an author, however, that Balso lusts for Mary, but as the archetypally desirable *shikse*, who—at the very moment his tongue is in her mouth—disconcertingly becomes "a middle-aged woman, dressed in a mannish suit and wearing horn-rimmed glasses," which is to say, Potiphar's wife turned schoolmarm. Once revealed, however, Miss McGeeney proves even less of a problem to Balso than her earliest prototype to Joseph: "He hit Miss McGeeney a terrific blow in the gut and hove her into the fountain." After which, she stays inside the limits of his fantasy, returning "warmly moist" to make possible the sexual climax with which the book ends, turning a dry dream wet.

More troublesome to Balso than his Gentile foster mother (to whom he can play Joseph or Oedipus, turn and turn about, with no real strain) is a kind of archetypal Jewish father, who disconcertingly appears in the very bowels of the horse, a self-appointed *kibbitzer* in the uniform of an official guide, from whom Balso has finally to wrench himself "with a violent twist," as the paternal busybody howls in his ear: "Sirrah . . . I am a Jew! and whenever anything Jewish is mentioned, I find it necessary to say that I am a Jew. I'm a Jew! A Jew!" It is the last such explicit declaration of Jewishness anywhere in West's work, on the lips of a character or in the words of the author himself; for after the exorcism of *Balso Snell,* his dreamers dream on presumably free forever of their aggressively Jewish censor. But the dreams that they dream—of Sodom burning, of the destruction of ever purer Josephs by ever grosser Potiphar's wives—we must call Jewish dreams.

Even the madness which cues them, we must call (more in sorrow than chauvinistic pride) Jewish madness; for just such madness, cuing just such dreams, we discover in that other great novel of the thirties, this time frankly Jewish in language and theme, Henry Roth's *Call It Sleep.* How aptly the ending of that book manages to catch, more in the rhythm, maybe, than in their manifest content, the phrasing of the words, that ambiguous moment at a day's end when it is uncertain whether the spirit is falling toward sleep and a dreaming from which it will wake with the morning or toward a total nightmare from which there is no waking ever. The cadences of that close and their hushed terror stay in my head, more than thirty years after Roth first conceived them, a valedictory both to his child protagonist in bed and to his own career as a writer: "He might as well call it sleep. It was only toward sleep that every wink of the eyelids could strike a spark into the cloudy tinder of the dark, kindle out of the shadowy corners of the bedoom such myriad and such vivid jets of images. . . ."

We know, having come so far in the novel, what those images "toward sleep" were, and are, obviously doomed to be until death for Roth and his protagonist: the adoring mother, exposed in her nakedness before jeering kids; the terrible rage of an actual Jewish father and the guilty dream of a *goyish* spiritual one; the Jewish girl betrayed in abject love to a mocking Gentile; the spark out of the bowels of the earth, up from the third electrified rail of the streetcar, bright enough to redeem all from darkness and pain; and, weaving in and out of the rest, the cry of the Prophet: "I am a man of unclean lips in the midst of a people of unclean lips. . . ."

Joseph—the solver of dreams—has become confused with Isaiah in the terrible thirties, learning to talk dirty instead of speaking fair; and he moves, therefore, not toward recognition and acclaim in his own lifetime and his father's, but like West or Roth, toward premature death or madness and silence. If, at long last, posthumous success has overtaken Nathanael West, and almost-posthumous acclaim Henry Roth—this is because the forties and fifties learned once more to believe in the Happy Ending, which the writers of Genesis postulated for the Joseph myth, but which the thirties could imagine no more than Kafka himself. The lowering into the pit, the descent into Egypt or Hell was all of the legend which seemed to them viable; and trapped in the darkness, they looked not to Pharaoh for deliverance, but to the psychoanalysts, the heirs of that Jewish Doctor who had boasted that he could set very Hell in motion.

In our time, however, with benefit of analysis or without, Joseph has once more been haled into Pharaoh's court, once more lifted up in the sight of his enemies and brothers; once more recognized as a true Master of Dreams, under his new names of J. D. Salinger and Bernard Malamud and Philip Roth and Saul Bellow. But this is the achievement of an era just now coming to a close, a decade or more of responsibility and accommodation, in which those erstwhile outsiders, Freud and Kafka, became assigned classroom reading, respectable topics for the popular press: an age which, rediscovering West and Roth, celebrated its own sons who had grown up reading them, the age of the Jew as winner. But how hard it is to love a winner—to love Bellow, let's say, after the National Book Award and best-sellerdom—in this land of ours, where nothing succeeds like failure, and all the world loves a loser.

How much more comfortable we feel with those exceptional figures of the forties-fifties who did not quite make it, dying too soon and still relatively unknown, like Isaac Rosenfeld, or surviving dimly inside of their wrecked selves until they could disappear unnoticed, like Delmore Schwartz. I, at least, find myself thinking often these days of Rosenfeld, who might well (it once seemed) have become our own Franz Kafka and who perhaps *was* (in a handful of stories like "The Pyramids" and "The Party," dreams of parables or parables of dreams) all the Kafka we shall ever have. And even more often my thoughts turn, ever since his pitiful death anyhow—in the same black year for the Jews which also saw Lenny Bruce go—to Delmore Schwartz, with whom the forties began two years before the official opening of the decade.

It was only 1938, even before the start of World War II, when there appeared a volume of his short fiction and verse called, appropriately enough, *In Dreams Begin Responsibilities*—"responsibilities" for the age to come, "dreams" for the long tradition on which he drew. In the title story, at any rate, a young man on the eve of his twenty-first birthday, is portrayed dreaming a dream that becomes a movie (not in technicolor, or even in black and white, but in gray on gray, those authentic Schwartzian colors), the movie of a dream. Asleep, but already on the verge of waking, he watches his parents, sundered by rage and mutual incomprehension before his birth or conception. " . . . and I keep shouting," he tells us, "What are they doing? Don't they know what they're doing? Why doesn't my mother go after my father?' . . . But the Usher has seized my arm and is dragging me away. . . ."

It is a nightmare uncannily apt for the Age of the Cold War and Going-to-the-Movies—an era whose chief discovery was disillusion: this bad dream of the past as irrevocably given and of the impotence of the young in the face of enormities which they inherit (and even understand) but cannot control. Born in reaction, it is a counterdream to the Marxian vision of apocalypse and social change which moved the thirties and of the hysterical despair which underlay it, the paranoia which its myth of the Class Struggle at once nurtured and concealed. But for the antipolitical politics of the forties-fifties, too, there is an appropriate psychosis, as there is for all brands of politics: the conviction of impotence freezing into catatonia—the total paralysis of the will of those with no place to go except *up* into the Counselor's seat at the right hand of the leaders of utterly corrupt states. Both the thirties and the forties-fifties, however, merely *suffered* varying forms of madness bred by Freud's Oedipal dream and the failure of Marxian politics.

It was left to the sixties (which got off to an even earlier start than most decades somewhere around 1955) to *celebrate* psychosis; and to attempt, for the first time, not to pretend that schizophrenia was politics, but to make a politics of schizophrenia recognized for what it is: a total and irrevocable protest against Things-as-They-Are in a world called real. And behind this movement, too, there is a Jewish dreamer, yet one more Joseph sufficient unto his day. I mean, of course, Allen Ginsberg who has escaped the hang-up of finding or not finding the ear of Pharaoh, by becoming a mock-Pharaoh, a Pharaoh of Misrule, as it were. Think of his actual presence at the head of parades or his image looking down at us from subway hoardings—crowned with the striped hat of Uncle Sam.

Ginsberg, however, unlike the Joseph before him, is no father's darling at all, not even such a baffled aspirant for paternal favor as was Kafka. He is a terminal son, to be sure, like the others—but a mama's boy this time, unable to imagine himself assuming papa's role ever ("Beep, emit a burst of babe and begone/ perhaps that's the answer, wouldn't know till you had a kid/ I dunno, never had a kid never will at the rate I'm going"), or saying *kaddish,* that traditional Jewish mourner's prayer which becomes an endearing synonym for "son"—except for his mother, called Naomi, and identified in his mythological imagination with her Biblical namesake, and with Ruth and Rebecca as well, though *not* with Rachel, that favored second wife of Jacob. She was a life-long Communist, that mother who haunts Ginsberg, who died—lobotomized and terror-stricken—in the nuthouse: "Back! You! Naomi! Skull on you! Gaunt immortality and revolution come—small broken woman— the ashen indoor eyes of hospitals, ward grayness on skin."

But her post-Marxian madness, the very paranoia which persuaded her that she had been shut away at the instigation of "Hitler, Grandma, Hearst, the Capitalists, Franco, Daily News, the 20's, Mussolini, the living dead," becomes in her son vision and a program fostered by that vision: "vow to illuminate mankind . . . (sanity a trick of agreement)." And when his own insanity fails to sustain him, he turns to drugs, singing—on marijuana and mescalin, Lysergic Acid and laughing gas and "Ayahusca, an Amazonian spiritual potion"—a New Song, appropriate to a new sort of Master of Dreams, the pusher's pusher, as it were. He does not sell the chemical stuff of dreams directly, of course (was this, then what the Jews *did* peddle in the market place of Juvenal's Rome?), but sells the notion of selling them—crying out in protest: "Marijuana is a benevolent narcotic but J. Edgar Hoover prefers his deathly scotch/And the heroin of Lao-Tze and the Sixth Patriarch is punished by the electric chair/but the poor sick junkies have nowhere to lay their heads. . . ." or insisting in hope: "The message is: Widen the area of consciousness."

The psychedelic revolution, however, whatever its affinities with the traditional Jewish trade of dream-pedlary and its appeal to the sons of Jewish merchants engaged in handling much harder goods, belongs to a world essentially *goyish:* the world of William Burroughs and Timothy Leary and (however little he might relish the thought) J.R.R. Tolkien. For a contemporary Master of Dreams more explicitly Joseph-ian, which is to say, Jewish, we must turn to a writer who in his own fantasies is never more than half-Jewish, to Norman Mailer. Those who have read the successive versions of his *The Deer Park* (or have seen it on the stage), and who know his most successful and impressive short stories, "The Man Who Studied Yoga" and "The Time of Her Time," as well as the notes on these in that mad compendium of self-pity and self-adulation, *Advertisements for Myself,* are aware that Mailer once planned a Great American Dream Novel in eight volumes.

Each volume, he tells us, was to have represented one of the "eight stages" in the dream of a defeated Jewish writer (Mailer makes him only one-quarter Jewish, which is to say, minimally though essentially so) called Sam Slavoda, who, in his nighttime fantasy sees himself as a kind of Super-Goy called Sergius O'Shaughnessy. In the dream of Slavoda, O'Shaughnessy, his heroic *alter ego,* is portrayed as eternally strugging with a Jewish father figure (in the recent dramatic version, we learn that he is "half-Jewish—on both sides"), named Eitel, for the possession of a Gentile girl, daughter or mistress or wife (essentially, I suppose, somebody else's wife, i.e., Potiphar's Wife), called Elena. It is all —thanks, alas, to Freud—distressingly explicit; and I for one was not, am not, sorry that the project ended in shipwreck and a ten years' silence; since out of that silence Mailer emerged to write a book less like Kafka and more like Pop Art—more indebted, that is, to the immediate Jewish past (those post-World War II Masters of Dreams, Shuster and Siegal, who inventing Superman for the comics, invented a possible future for the dying novel) than to a remoter one no longer viable.

That book is, of course, *An American Dream,* in which dreamer and dream-actor have become one, Sam Slavoda plus Sergius O'Shaughnessy turning into Stephen Rojack—who is half-Jewish, since in the world of myth a quarter Jew plus a full Gentile equals a half-Jew. But he is precisely the half-Jew, the half of Joseph, that neither Kafka nor the great writers of the thirties could envision: Joseph *after* his recognition, the very archetype of the Man Who Has Made it. No protagonist has entered our recent fiction with so impressive a list of distinctions, for he is a Congressman, a decorated War Hero, the friend of a future President of the United States, the M.C. of a successful T.V. program; as well as a tireless cocksman, who can get away with murdering his own wife, then walk the parapet of a penthouse under the eye of his evil Fascist father-in-law, turn down that Bad Father's homosexual advances, and triumph finally over a Total Conspiracy—in which all of his Bad Brothers (transformed fashionably into members of the Mafia and the C.I.A.) have joined with that Father to destroy him.

Mailer's latest book is, indeed, in its very banality and vulgarity just such an American Dream as its title advertises it to be; but it is also a Jewish Dream: if not Joseph's own dream, at least our dream of Joseph, as well as a Jewish interpretation of the dreams of Pharaoh's (read "John F. Kennedy's") servants. Try as he will, therefore, Mailer cannot basically alter the shape of the myth he has inherited. How desperately he yearns to permit his Joseph (unlike the earlier Josephs from whom he descends) to have all that glory and Potiphar's Wife, too—in fact, all three of the Gentile women into whom Mailer has split the single figure of the original legend. But, in the end, Rojack has to reject them like the Josephs before him, so that his soul may live. Deborah Coughlin Mangravede Kelly he marries and kills, though—or maybe because—she is Pharaoh's Wife rather than Potiphar's. Mailer nowhere says outright, of course, that she is intended to be a portrait of Jacqueline Kennedy; but she reminds us of the mythological Jackie at least. And Rojack, introducing her, explains, "Forgive me, I thought the road to President might begin at the entrance to her Irish heart."

And the mistress once dead, he must destroy the maid who is her extension, too: penetrating all three of her entrances, one by one, but reaching his climax—and cheating her of her own—in the *Anus Mirabilis* (we are back to Balso Snell once more, and this time the identification is explicitly made between asshole and Acheron: "I had come to the Devil a fraction too late, and nothing had been there to receive me. . . ."). Buggery is the essential aspect of a sexual connection whose aim is annihilation not fulfillment; and buggery extorts from the red-headed German Ruta, the confession that she had been a Nazi: " 'Ja.' She shook her head. 'No, no,' she went on. 'Ja, don't stop, ja.' ' After which Rojack is able to declare, "There was a high private pleasure in plugging a Nazi, there was something clean despite all. . . ."

But another third of Potiphar's wife remains to be dealt with; after the Irish aristocrat and the Kraut servant, the ultimately blonde, all-American Wasplet: the Happy Ending Girl, whose name, Cherry, declares, I suppose, that whatever befalls her flesh, mythologically she remains eternally virgin. Cherry, Rojack truly loves, but her, too, he leads to her death—involuntarily, but inevitably all the same; not, however, until he has won her in an archetypal battle with a *really* Bad Brother—a Negro junkie who comes at him with a knife. It is as if Mailer were trying to declare, or his fable in his despite: "Things haven't changed all that much, my colored brothers; a Jewish boy in good condition can still beat out you spade hipsters in the struggle for that archetypal blonde *shikse* who embodies the American psyche." Yet in the end, the spades who cannot keep her in life do her in; the friends of the hipster whom Rojack has earlier defeated, humiliated, in effect, *killed,* destroy our poor Cherry. And Rojack, guiltless of that murder, is released from the burden of actual love—releasing his author at the same moment from all obligations to realism: liberating him into the world if not of pure myth, at least of Pop Art fantasy.

As the book closes, Mailer asks us to believe, Rojack has stopped at a disconnected phone booth in the middle of the Great American Desert; and when he dials (sleeping or waking, we are not sure) the voice of his dead beloved answers—and why not, after all. "Why, hello hon, I thought you'd never call. . . . Marilyn says to say hello." At this point, Mailer's personal fantasy becomes once more our common fantasy, his dream girl ours, as Cherry blends into our own late, perhaps too much lamented, Marilyn Monroe; and somehow we are supposed to be, somehow we *are* at peace. It is a long way from the beginning of Mailer's book to the end: from his evocation of the dead Dream Boy of us all (the novel opens, "I met Jack Kennedy in November, 1946. We were both war heroes and had been elected to Congress"), whose death one crazy Jew, himself now dead, thought he was avenging—to the Dead Dream Girl of us all, of whose death another saner Jew has written a play to prove himself guiltless. But it is a way which leads from madness to sanity, from falling asleep to waking up; from the lunatic wish to be President and screw all the women in the world, to the modest hope of finding someone to love and the resolve to take time out for thinking things over.

"But in the morning," Stephen Rojack ends by saying, "I was something like sane again, and packed the car and started on the long trip to Guatemala and Yucatan." Maybe this, too, is only one more fantasy, the last madness of believing oneself sane; or maybe Joseph *is* sane again, at least as Mailer has re-imagined, re-embodied him; maybe, in exorcising himself of the American Dream, the American version of the flight from Potiphar's wife, Mailer has healed himself—demonstrating that artist and doctor can inhabit the same head. Didn't Freud himself assert (apropos of his own at-

tempt along the same lines, the very book with which we began)
that successful self-analysis is possible to one who is "a prolific
enough dreamer"?

But even granting all this, we are left with the final question:
what does this mean to *us?* What do Joseph's personal healing and
his consequent success (after all, *An American Dream* did prove a
best-seller, and more, a way back into writing again for its author)
mean to those who have helped make that success, critics or readers
or nonreading buyers of books? And the answer to that question I
have been pursuing throughout—reflecting on how the Jewish
Dreamer in Exile, thinking only of making his own dreams come
true, ends by deciphering the alien dreams of that world as well;
thus determining the future of all those who can only know what
lies before them dimly and in their sleep. It is the essence of the
myth I have been exploring that Joseph, the Master of Dreams,
cannot lie; for dreams tell only the truth, and the Dreamer is also a
Dream. But the final word on the subject has been said by Freud
himself, in his peroration to *The Interpretation of Dreams:*

> The ancient belief that dreams reveal the future is not entirely
> devoid of truth. By representing a wish as fulfilled the dream
> certainly leads us into the future; but this future, which the
> dreamer accepts as his present, has been shaped in the likeness
> of the past by an indestructible wish.

Buffalo, N. Y.
—1967

INDEX

Index